# Bridging Mathematics, Philosophy and Theology

**What They Say......**

Clear thinking can benefit from fuzzy logic. Binoy Jacob Pichalakkattu demonstrates how critical realism in both science and theology complement one another as our finite human minds attempt to grasp penultimate and ultimate reality. This is a creative breakthrough treatment.

**Ted Peters, Co-Editor**
***Theology and Science***
**CTNS (Centre for Theology and the Natural Sciences)**
**USA**

The author has made a scholarly attempt to make use of mathematics (fuzzy logic) as language while interfacing science and theology. It is, no doubt, a great piece!

**Javier Leach**
**Former Professor of Mathematics and Logic**
**Complutense University**
**Spain**

Excellent job, good argumentation, readable procedure, and promising outputs for a future implementation

**Jozef Fekete**
**Professor of Philosophy**
**University of Trnava**
**Slovakia**

The application of fuzzy logic to theology - with or without specifying particular cumulative distributions - will make a significant contribution to interfaith dialogues if the partners take it to be an honest (not a trap), solid (not shaky or slippery), safe (not dangerous), serious (not a joke) alternative to true-false dogmatism.

**Carlos E. Vasco**
**Professor Emeritus of Mathematics**
**National University of Colombia**
**Colombia**

# Bridging Mathematics, Philosophy and Theology

## Fuzzy Logical Thinking for Science-Religion Dialogue

**Binoy Pichalakkattu SJ**

CWI
Christian World Imprints(TM)

First Published in 2017 by

**Christian World Imprints**(TM)
*Christian Publishing & Books from India*
H-12 Bali Nagar, **New Delhi-110015**
info@christianworldimprints.com
www.ChristianWorldImprints.com
Phone: +91 11 25465925

ISBN: 978-93-5148-211-6 (HB) ISBN: 978-93-5148-212-3 (PB)

**Cataloging in Publication Data--DK**
Courtesy: D.K. Agencies (P) Ltd. <docinfo@dkagencies.com>

**Pichalakkattu, Binoy, author.**
Bridging mathematics, philosophy and theology : fuzzy logical thinking for science-religion dialogue / Binoy Pichalakkattu SJ.
pages cm
ISBN 9789351482116 (HB)
ISBN 9789351482123 (PB)

1. Fuzzy logic--Religious aspects. 2. Religion and science. 3. Theology. I. Title.

BL240.3.P53 2017 DDC 215 23



**Printed in India.**

To My Beloved Parents:
Jacob and Annakutty

# Contents

# Foreword

More and more people, both at the popular and academic levels, are convinced of the need for creative and critical dialogue between science and religion. Such a dialogue is essential for the future of humanity.

This book by Dr. Binoy Pichalakkattu is an attempt to place such a dialogue in the framework of fuzzy logic.

The book argues that a fuzzy model of critical realism will provide a mathematical base to overcome the binary thinking without indulging in reductionism and relativism. The author believes the model offered by fuzzy logic will provide an inclusive epistemological framework for science-theology dialogue where multiple referential claims reinforce each other. The book delineates the possibilities of fuzzy thinking vis-a-vis binary, relativist and probabilistic thinking. It also brings to light the limitations of fuzzy logic and fuzzy model of critical realism. The book ends by suggesting some directions for exploring fuzzy thinking in religion and developing a fuzzy language for talking about God and religion. Such an attempt enables a deeper and creative way of dealing with science and religion, theology and philosophy.

After explaining the insights of fuzziness in a way understandable to the popular audience, the author highlights the significance of critical realism as a starting point to encounter reality. Then he applies the rich mathematical insights from fuzzy logic and provides a new and dynamic model for science-theology interaction. Such an attempt, I am convinced, is essential for developing a fertile ground for meaningful science-religion dialogue.

While wishing the author all success, I hope that the movement of science-religion dialogue will bring about abundant fruits for the whole of humanity.

**Prof Kuruvilla Pandikattu SJ**
Dean, Faculty of Philosophy
Jnana-Deepa Vidyapeeth
Pune 411014
www.kuru.in
March 8, 2017

# Acknowledgement

This book owes special debt of gratitude to many:

Prof. Dr. Robert John Russell and Prof. Dr. Ted Peters (CTNS-Center for Theology and the Natural Sciences, Berkeley); Dr. Thomas Cattoi (Santa Clara University, California); Dr. Fady Chidiac (University of California, Berkeley); the American Jesuit Assistancy and the Clavius Group of Catholic mathematicians, U.S.A.

I have benefited much from the extensive discussions with a number of scholars like Prof. Dr. K. Babu Joseph (Former Vice Chancellor, Cochin University of Science and Technology); Prof. Dr. K. K. Jose (Former Principal, St. Thomas College, Pala); Prof. Dr. Job Kozhamthadam (Indian Institute of Science and Religion, Delhi); Prof. Dr. Kuruvilla Pandikattu (Jnana-Deepa Vidyapeeth, Pune) and Dr. Augustine Pamplany (Institute of Science and Religion, Aluva).

This work would not have been possible without the continuous encouragement and support extended by my superiors and friends in the Kerala Province of the Society of Jesus.

1 May 2017

Gratefully ever,

**Binoy Pichalakkattu SJ**
Loyola Institute of Peace and
International Relations (LIPI), Kochi, India.
Pin: 682 017
email: binoysj@gmail.com
www.lipijesuits.org, www.ezhuthu.org

# Figures

# Glossary

***a posteriori***: Way of reasoning from known events than assumptions.

***a priori***: Way of reasoning based on theoretical deduction than empirical observation.

***Aham Brahmasmi***: "I am Brahman" is from one of the Mahavakyas from Brihadaranyaka Upanishad (1.4.10). It explains the unity of macrocosm and microcosm.

**Axiom**: Self-evident proposition that needs no proof.

**Binary number**: A number expressed in the base-2 numeral system which represents numeric values using the symbol of 0 and 1.

**Classical mathematics**: The mainstream approach to mathematics based on classical logic (Aristotelian logic). It allows proofs by finding contradictions in opposites.

**Completeness**: There are no true propositions which cannot be proved in the system implying that only true propositions can be proven within the system.

**Consistency**: No two theorems within a mathematical system can contradict one another implying that all true propositions can be proved within the system.

**Cosmotheandric**: The integrated vision of the reality and the undivided consciousness of the totality: God, human and the world.

**Critical realism**: The view in which reality is both mind-dependent and mind-independent.

**Epistemology**: Theory of knowledge which includes the study of the nature and method of knowledge.

**Eternity**: Refers to infinite or unending time. Theologically it means life after death.

**First-order predicate logic**: A fundamental formal system of logic that included a domain of discourse by defining functions and relations on the elements of this domain.

**Formal language**: A language consisting of well-defined series of signs than ordinary words. It is the language of logic, mathematics and computer science.

**Formal logic**: Set of rules for making deductions that seems self evident.

**Fuzzy Logic**: Precise mathematics that deals with various kinds of fuzziness that exist in the real world such as vagueness, impreciseness, uncertainty, and ambiguity.

**Hermeneutics**: Branch of knowledge that deals with interpretation.

**Law of contradiction**: A logical principle which states that a thing cannot at the same time both be and not be.

**Law of excluded middle**: A principle in logic which states that for any proposition, either that proposition is true or its negation is true.

**Logic**: The science of correct reasoning based on formal laws.

**Mathematics**: Pure mathematics is an abstract science that deals with abstract concepts like number, quantity, space, etc. It has four traditional branches namely arithmetic, geometry, algebra and analysis. Geometry is concerned with the study of lines, shapes, angles and their properties. Algebra is a branch of mathematics that substitutes letters for numbers. Arithmetic usually refers to four operations of positive numbers: addition, subtraction, multiplication and division. Analysis is the branch of mathematics that deals with limits and related theories like differentiation and integration. Applied mathematics is the application of pure mathematics to other disciplines.

**Membership function**: A curve that defines how each input in the universe of discourse is mapped to a value called degree of membership.

**Metaphysics**: Branch of philosophy that deals with the fundamental principles of reality.

**Philosophy**: Study of the fundamental nature of reality, knowledge, truth, existence, meaning, etc.

**Probability**: The measure of likelihood; the extent to which something is likely to occur.

**Realism**: The view that reality is independent of our mind and perceptions.

**Religion**: A system of belief and worship. Code, creed, cult and community are its constitutive factors.

**Set theory**: Branch of mathematics that deals with formal properties of sets. Set is a well-defined collection of distinct objects.

**Statistics**: Branch of mathematics that deals with the collection, analysis, interpretation and organization of data.

**Syntax**: The arrangement of words in a sentence, defining particular ways they modify each other.

***Tat Tvam Asi***: "That you are" is one of the Mahavakyas from Chandogya Upanishad (6.8.7), one of the twelve major Upanishads.

**Theology**: Systematic study of the nature of God, religious belief and practices.

**Theorem**: In mathematics, theorem is a proposition that is not self-evident and hence must be proved. Theory in science is different from mathematical theorem as scientific theories are considered valid only after testing the hypothesis.

**Trinity**: The Christian doctrine that holds one God in three persons.

# Prologue

"Science can purify religion from error and superstition; religion can purify science from idolatry and false absolutes. Each can draw the other into a wider world, a world in which both can flourish."[1]

-Pope John Paul II

I have been engaged in the dialogue between science and theology for well over the past nine years. Many times I have come across people - children, adults and grown-ups - asking whether science and theology are incompatible with each other. Most of them think that conflict between these two disciplines is inevitable. This book, in general, aims at fostering science-theology dialogue and in particular, provides a 'fuzzy logical' explanation of critical realism for the methodological bridging between science and theology. My interest in method, especially in critical realism, developed in the fall of 2011 after having conversations with Robert John Russell and Ted Peters at the Center for Theology and the Natural Sciences (CTNS), Berkeley, California. With methodological clarity, both science and theology can better enhance each other and ultimately all humanity irrespective of class, caste, creed or religion.

---

i. John Paul II, *Letter to the Reverend George V. Coyne, S.J., Director of Vatican Observatory*, 1 June, 1988, cited in *Physics, Philosophy and Theology: A Common Quest for Understanding*, ed. Robert John Russell, William R. Stoeger and George V. Coyne, S.J. (Vatican City: Vatican Observatory Publications, 1988), M 13.

Finding an adequate method has been an important area of concern ever since the beginning of the science-theology interface. Many scholars have contributed to the use of critical realism, a philosophical theory that asserts the mind-dependent and mind-independent aspects of reality, as a methodological bridge between science and theology. This means that some of our sense-data can accurately represent external objects, properties, and events, while some sense-data do not accurately represent any external objects, properties, and events. Some scholars define critical realism within a modern epistemological framework. Others define it within a postmodern epistemological framework. In spite of these efforts to define critical realism, epistemological concerns remain in various modes while relating science and theology. In this book, I define critical realism within a fuzzy logical framework to improve upon the prevailing explanations of it in science-theology dialogue.

Fuzzy logic has often been wrongly criticized as "fuzzy" or "vague" due to the use of the word "fuzzy." In reality, fuzzy logic is precise mathematics that deals with non-linear and uncertain situations. The logical tool itself is clear and not ambiguous. The research will illustrate how the fuzzy logical method can be effectively applied in theology as well as in science-theology dialogue.

I will argue that a fuzzy model of critical realism will provide a mathematical base to overcome the binary thinking without indulging in reductionism and relativism. I will also argue that this model will offer an inclusive epistemological framework for science-theology dialogue where multiple referential claims reinforce one another.

To address the epistemological concerns in the methodological bridging between science and theology, a single critical realist epistemological framework based on fuzzy logic is introduced. Fuzzy logic, developed by Lofti A. Zadeh at the University of California, Berkeley, in 1965, deals with different kinds of fuzziness such as uncertainty, complexity, incompleteness, imprecision, non-specificity and vagueness. This way of dealing with fuzzy situations is to claim that there are degrees of truth that are typically represented by the real numbers in the interval [0, 1]. The extreme points 0 and 1 represent absolute falsity and absolute truth, while the values in between represent intermediate truth degrees. Mathematical equations and graphical representations are used to explain the fuzzy logical categories such as fuzzy sets, membership functions, and fuzzy numbers, which better represent the events in life.

The fuzzy logical explanation of critical realism raises two probelmatic research questions: (i) How well does fuzzy logic apply to the historically developed problems of critical realism? (ii) How well does the fuzzy logical explanation of critical realism apply to theology within the matrix of science-theology dialogue? The mathematical model of fuzzy logic is not applied directly to theology, but an adaptive model based on the epistemology of fuzzy logic is used to enhance science-theology dialogue.

The book will unfold in this manner: First, I will deal with critical realism, specifically the diverse use of critical realism in the methodological bridging between science and theology. Next, I make a detailed inquiry into the critical realist views of Ian G. Barbour (methodological parallels) and Arthur Peacocke (epistemic emergence) and Nancey Murphy (Imre Lakatos' theory of scientific method). Murphy regards Barbour's and Peacocke's explanations of critical realism as modern, and against them she provides a postmodern explanation of critical realism. I claim that Murphy's postmodern explanation against the critical realist views of Barbour and Peacocke requires a careful construction of epistemology. In response, I will introduce a fuzzy model of critical realism to fit multiple referential claims together into a conceptual web which reinforce each other.

The following chapters develop the findings of the study. First, it is claimed that a fuzzy model of critical realism addresses the binary-relativist trends by adding more levels of intermediate truth values to the idea of absolutes. With the help of a two dimensional (2D) coordinate system, how the fuzzy model of critical realism enhances science-theology dialogue within a single critical realist and fuzzy framework is demonstrated. In this model, the correspondence theory of truth is not replaced but complemented by a coherence version of truth. Reference to the external or objective world is retained, while subjective constructivism is acknowledged as integral to it in a single act of human knowing.

Next, the fuzzy model of critical realism is applied to three pertinent examples. In the first application, with reference to the study of Robert John Russell is provided a fuzzy logical framework for time in eternity, and eternity in time. In the second application, with reference to the views of Basil of Caesarea (330 CE - 379 CE) and Gregory of Nyssa (335 CE – 394 CE), it is shown that fuzzy thinking can efficiently address the Trinitarian paradox of "unity with distinction." In the third application, based on the views of Raimon Panikkar and Paul F. Knitter, it is explained that, contrary to binary thinking, in fuzzy thinking, religions can sensibly make their claims to uniqueness.

The closing chapter deals with the possibilities of fuzzy logic in comparison with binary, relativist and probabilistic thinking. It also brings to light the limitations of fuzzy logic and fuzzy model of critical realism. The study ends by suggesting a few possibilities for exploring fuzzy thinking in religions and developing a fuzzy language for talking about God and religions.

The work is significant from the point of view of method. According to Vatican Council II, "Methodological research in all branches of knowledge, provided it is carried on in a truly scientific manner and in accordance with moral norms, can never conflict with faith, because the things of the world and things of faith derive from the same God."[2] The method applied in this work, in general, is critical realism. Critical realism affirms the role of mental construction and imaginative activity in the formation of models and theories. The theory of fuzzy logic and the fuzzy model of critical realism provide a mathematical basis

ii Vatican II, *Gaudium et Spes*, no. 36.

for comprehending the uncertainties and ambiguities associated with the human cognitive processes of thinking and reasoning both in science and theology. As a result, fuzzy thinking provides an adequate conceptual framework for science and theology to engage in dialogue and to address the complex realities of human life.

Finally, I find fuzzy thinking and fuzzy language highly promising in the multi-religious and multicultural context of India to promote interreligious dialogue and peaceful co-existence. This view is epitomized in the classical statement of Albert Einstein, "Science without religion is lame and religion without science is blind."[3]

The present study has its own limitations too. Fuzzy logic itself experiences limitations due to methodological, linguistic and practical complexities. It is important to acknowledge that I have used both the terms, postmodern and modern, in ways that are different from the standard usage of these terms. So too with the use of the scientific term non-linear. To be precise, in this investigation, the fuzzy model of critical realism focuses only on overcoming the binary thinking and offering a holistic epistemological framework for the methodological bridging between science and theology. A fuzzy logical approach may not offer a one-off remedy to any question that arises during the methodological bridging. Instead, this approach devises an open-ended decision tool that can continue to improve as time goes on and as circumstances change.

---

iii Albert Einstein, *Out of My Later Years* (New York: Philosophical Library, 1950), 26.

# 1. Critical Realism

What is critical realism? Critical realism, in general, is a theory of knowledge. It makes epistemological claims regarding how we know things that we can and cannot see. In the realist view, reality is mind-independent. In the critical realist view, reality is both mind-dependent and mind-independent. As a form of realism, it presupposes that it is possible to know the external world as it is, independent of the human mind. As critical, it presupposes that human subjectivity and mental construction enable to know the objective world. Many scholars have used different forms of critical realism. In this chapter, we focus mainly on critical realism as used in science-theology dialogue. The chapter begins with a brief historical overview of critical realism based on the views of the British philosopher, Roy Bhaskar and ends by critically appraising the use of critical realism in science-theology dialogue.

## 1.1 Critical Realism: A Brief Historical Overview

Critical realism emerged as a powerful philosophical movement after the publication of Roy Bhaskar's *A Realist Theory of Science* in 1975.[1] The term "critical realism" elides the phrases

1 Roy Bhaskar, *A Realist Theory of Science,* 2nd edition (London: Routledge, 2008). The origin of critical realism cannot be attributed to Bhaskar alone, as the term 'critical realism' was first coined by Roy Wood Sellars in 1915 to refer to an approach to scientific naturalism that stood in contrast to idealism, pragmatism and realism. Sellars' ideas are published in the 1920 collection by

"transcendental realism" and "critical naturalism," used by Bhaskar in his *A Realist Theory of Science* and *The Possibility of Naturalism*.[2] The word "critical" suggests its association with Kant's philosophy, while 'realism' indicates its distance from it.

### 1.1.1 Transcendental Realism

Transcendental Realism emerged in the context of critiquing the positivism that dominated the philosophy of science at the beginning of the twentieth century. Specifically, it aimed at critically assessing the views of the 1920s - 1930s Vienna circle, dominated by logical positivism, which regarded science as absolutely empiricist, reductionist, rational and determinate.[3] Transcendental realism regards objects of knowledge as the structures and mechanisms that generate phenomena, and sees knowledge as a social product. Bhaskar states, "These objects [of knowledge] are neither phenomena (empiricism) nor human constructs imposed upon the phenomena (idealism), but real structures which endure and operate independently of our knowledge, our experience and the conditions which allow us access to them."[4]

Bhaskar introduces three kinds of ontological depth to transcendental realism: *intransitivity, transfactuality and stratification*.[5] He explains the *intransitivity* of knowledge in relation to its transitive dimension. The transitive dimension of knowledge refers to material causes which include antecedently established knowledge, theories, paradigms, models, methods and techniques of inquiry available to a particular scientific

Durant Drake, *Essay in Critical Realism: A Co-operative Study of the Problem of Knowledge* (London: Macmillan, 1920).

2 Roy Bhaskar, "General Introduction," in *Critical Realism: Essential Readings*, ed. Margaret Archer, Roy Bhaskar, Andrew Collier, Tony Lawson and Alan Norrie (London: Routledge, 1998), ix.

3 Archer, *Critical Realism*, x.

4 Bhaskar, *A Realist Theory of Science*, 15.

5 Archer, *Critical Realism*, xi.

school to generate new knowledge.[6] The intransitive dimension exceeds the transitive dimension, affirming the irreducible and extra-experimental character of science. Transitive knowledge depends upon antecedent knowledge and the efficient activity of humans; on the other hand, intransitive knowledge depends upon neither, existing quite independently of humans. The intransitive dimension of knowledge sustains the social character of science as well as the independent existence and activity of causal structures and things.[7]

*Transfactuality* refers to how "the laws of nature operate independently of the closure or otherwise of the systems in which they occur."[8] In an open system, causal laws can be universal "if they are interpreted in a transfactual (non-empirical) way, i.e., as designating the activity of generative mechanisms and structures independently of any particular sequence or pattern of events."[9] According to Bhaskar, "The laws then are neither empirical statements (statements about experiences) nor statements about events. Rather they are statements about the ways of acting of independently existing and transfactually active things."[10]

In Bhaskar's view, *stratification* occurs both in nature and in science. For Bhaskar, reality is stratified at three levels: the empirical (level of experience), actual (level of events) and real (level of structures and causal laws).[11] In science, stratification occurs within a single science or subject matter and between a series of them.[12] Science, for Bhaskar, must be conceived "as an ongoing process of transformation, continually or essentially in motion, in an attempt to capture (i.e. penetrate and describe) the

---

6 Ibid., 11.

7 Bhaskar, *A Realist Theory of Science*, 14.

8 Archer, *Critical Realism*, xii.

9 Bhaskar, *A Realist Theory of Science*, 3.

10 Ibid., 42.

11 Archer, *Critical Realism*, 41.

12 Bhaskar, *A Realist Theory of Science*, 54.

stratification of the world."[13] He says, "Without the concept of real strata apart from our knowledge of strata we could not make sense of what the scientist, striving to move from knowledge of one stratum to knowledge of the next, is trying to do."[14] According to Bhaskar, "The acknowledgement of the real stratification of the world allows us to reconcile scientific discovery (of new strata) with scientific change (of knowledge of strata)."[15] Bhaskar's concept of stratification is highly critical of any exclusively formal account of science in general and the deductive view of the structure of scientific theories in particular.

### 1.1.2 Critical Naturalism

The aim of Bhaskar's *The Possibility of Naturalism* is to transcend the dichotomies and dualisms that dominated the scientific and philosophical worldviews of the twentieth century. Primarily it addresses the question whether society in general and the human person in particular, could be studied in the same way as nature; that is, scientifically. Basically this question is rooted in *naturalism* which is defined by "an essential unity of method between the natural and the social sciences."[16] Critical naturalism is both a critical and non-reductionist form of naturalism, based upon a transcendental realist account of science in relation to the social realm. Bhaskar explains critical naturalism as follows:

> On the new critical naturalism that emerges, justice is done both to the *conceptuality* (or concept-dependence) and to the *transfactuality* (or generality) of the subject-matter of social science. The production of meaning is seen as law-governed but not determined; and the conceptual activity of social agents as at once both necessary for, and necessitated by, social structures and subject to critique

13 Bhaskar, *A Realist Theory of Science*, 176.

14 Ibid., 161.

15 Ibid., 162.

16 Roy Bhaskar, *The Possibility of Naturalism*, 3rd edition (London: Routledge, 1998), 3.

> both for what it presents and for what it obscures. Now such an explanatory critique is itself a moment in the process it describes. So that social science, on this conception, is critical, self-reflexive and totalizing. And its objects are existentially, but not causally, intransitive; concept dependent, but not conceptual; and transfactually efficacious, but irreducibly historical; that is, bound in space and restricted in time.[17]

The concepts of transcendental realism and critical naturalism help Bhaskar to construct a realist theory of science. His "transcendental" condition for experience lies in those mechanisms and structures of the "external" world independent of the human mind, which science discovers. Thus, reality becomes both mind-dependent and mind-independent (critically realist). Bhaskar's work exhibits two phases in the development of critical realism. The first phase opened up a non-reductionist and non-positivist account of humans and science, whereas, the second phase introduced a dialectical understanding of critical realism in relation to Hegelian and Marxist insights.[18]

## 1.2 Critical Realism in Science

Science requires extra-scientific reality in order to be science.[19] Critical realism in science asserts this extra-scientific reality in scientific inquiry and scientific knowledge. Scientific knowledge rests upon certain fundamental axiomatic assumptions about the nature of reality. Every scientific inquiry is characterized by a fundamental trust in the correspondence between the order of nature and the order of mind. The correspondence that exists between the objective physical world of nature outside and the

17 Bhaskar, *The Possibility of Naturalism*, 136.

18 Roy Bhaskar, *Dialectic: The Pulse of Freedom,* 2nd edition (London: Routledge, 2008).

19 Peters and Peterson calls the extra-scientific reality in science "faith." Ted Peters and Carl Peterson, "The Higgs Boson: An Adventure in Critical Realism," *Theology and Science*, vol. 11, no. 3 (2013): 185.

subjective mental world of mind inside cannot be demonstrated or proved within science. Such a correspondence is an extra-scientific reality. English physicist, Paul Davies, trusts in this extra-scientific reality in scientific knowledge. Davies says, "Sooner or later we all have to accept something as given, whether it is God, or logic, or a set of laws, or some other foundation for existence. Thus, ultimate questions will always lie beyond the scope of empirical science as it is usually defined."[20]

The extra-scientific reality in science can be verified mathematically. In the 1930s, Austrian Kurt Gödel, one of the greatest logicians of all time, proved a couple of revolutionary mathematical theorems, now known as *Gödel's incompleteness theorems.* The first incompleteness theorem says that "any consistent axiomatic system, rich enough to be of mathematical interest, will have recognizably true sentences that are not provable in the system in question."[21] This means that an axiomatic formalized consistent system is incomplete.[22] The second incompleteness theorem states that "any consistent system of sufficient complexity to be of mathematical interest cannot prove its own consistency."[23] It implies that the consistency within a system cannot be proved by the arithmetic. In other words, the truth of the axioms as well as the truth of the true statements of any scientific system cannot be proved within the system. It is inherently necessary to leave a system and enter a higher and richer system to prove the truth

20 Paul Davies, *The Mind of God: The Scientific Basis for a Rational World* (New York: Simon and Schuster, 1992), 15.

21 Mark Colyvan, *An Introduction to the Philosophy of Mathematics* (Cambridge: Cambridge University Press, 2012), 27.

22 Consistency means no two theorems within a system can contradict one another. A contradictory theorem cannot be derived in the theory. It implies, all true propositions can be proved within the system. Completeness means there are no true propositions which cannot be proved in the system which means only true propositions can be proven within the system. For details, refer to Michat Walicki, *Introduction to Mathematical Logic* (Singapore: World Scientific, 2012), 35-36.

23 Colyvan, *Introduction*, 27.

of the given system. This means that the truth of the axioms of a system exists at a meta-level and scientists trust these axioms in "faith."

The key to critical realism is the formulation of conceptual or theoretical models, mostly mathematical, to assess data and organize measurements. British physical cosmologist, Stephen Hawking, refers to model construction as model-dependent realism.[24] According to Hawking, "A physical theory or world picture is a model (generally of a mathematical nature) and a set of rules that connect the elements of the model to observations."[25] Models relate empirical data to physical reality. Science demands more extra-scientific realities when a scientist posits the existence of a physical reality on the basis of a conceptual model, even though empirical evidence for that reference is insufficient. Ian G. Barbour, an eminent American physicist, describes the realist and imaginative content of models and theories in science. In his view, critical realism "affirms the role of mental construction and imaginative activity in the formation of theories, and it asserts that some constructs agree with observations better than others only because events have an objective pattern."[26] Barbour brings to light, along with human imagination, the socio-cultural and linguistic influences on theory formulation and model development.

British biochemist, Arthur Peacocke, explains the basic claim of critical realism in science in relation to the use of metaphors:

> For the basic claim made by such a critical scientific realism is that it is the long-term success of a scientific theory that warrants the belief that something like the entities and structure postulated by the theory actually exists....It must never be forgotten that the realism is

24 Stephen Hawking and Leonard Mlodinow, *The Grand Design* (New York: Bantam Books, 2010), 7.

25 Hawking, *The Grand Design*, 43.

26 Ian G. Barbour, *Issues in Science and Religion* (San Francisco: Harper and Row, 1966), 172.

> always qualified as 'critical' since the language of science is...fundamentally metaphorical and revisable, while nevertheless referring....this position of critical realism as regards the status of scientific propositions inevitably involves some theory of reference.[27]

Critical realism in science acknowledges that extra-scientific reality is fundamental to any scientific inquiry and scientific knowledge. Ted Peters and Carl Peterson illustrate how critical realism (extra-scientific reality) is being used in the recent scientific expedition for the Higgs boson. Nearly five decades ago, physicists hypothesized the existence of a particle responsible for providing mass to other particles. This meant that the standard model of fundamental particles and forces explaining the make-up of ordinary matter, was missing something. In 2012, researchers in Switzerland working with the giant high-energy particle accelerator, the Large Hadron Collider (LHC), announced they had found it. The standard model required the existence of such a component, even though it had not yet been empirically detected. Peters and Peterson write:

> The problem with this standard model in its initial development was that it is a theory for particles with zero mass. The mass question remained unanswered. Somehow, it seemed, mass would have to emerge from interactions of the otherwise massless particles. This led to the hypothesis that the empty space would be filled with a field, a scalar field that is always present, and named the Higgs field--after Peter Higgs and associated with a quantum, the Higgs boson.... The concept of the Higgs field was introduced to break the symmetry of one of the mathematical theories used in the standard model, thereby allowing the particles to gain the mass.[28]

27 Arthur Peacocke, *Theology for a Scientific Age* (Minneapolis: Fortress Press, 1993), 12-13.

28 Peters and Peterson, "The Higgs Boson," 187-188.

Peters and Peterson further delineate the various steps (collecting, examining and correlating data, developing and testing hypotheses, stating a theory and submitting findings for peer review and publication) involved in the scientific search for the Higgs boson and affirm this search as a clear case of critical realism:

> The boson was predicted to exist for the purpose of giving mass to particles in the standard model. The standard model is a mathematical formulation that describes coherently how the various particles in it fit together. Empirical evidence had been provided for particles with mass in SM; but the theory would remain malnourished until it could imbibe evidence for particle mass. The Higgs boson mathematical structure was needed, paraphrasing Hawking, to set the rules that connect the particles in the model to experimental reality.[29]

The Higgs boson experiment substantiates the critical realist approach in science. In spite of the inadequacy of models, scientists require and trust the model method for further scientific exploration. The use of metaphors, the imaginative content in models and theories, and the socio-cultural, historical and linguistic influences on them illustrate the use of critical realism (extra-scientific reality) in science.

## 1.3 Critical Realism in Science-Theology Dialogue

Can the critical realist stance from science be adopted for theological explorations? Critical realism in science and critical realism in theology share something in common; namely, neither can see their referential object directly--whether it be a sub-atomic particle like the Higgs boson or God--so this method constructs conceptual models to describe what cannot be perceived directly. The models presuppose a referent, but they emit indirect rather

29 Ibid., 189.

than direct knowledge. For Knut-Willy Saether, philosopher of religion at the Norwegian School of Leadership and Theology, scientific critical realism is not directly transferable to theology. He says, "Both science and theology aim to say something about the same world. This means critical realism in science is not directly transferred to theology, but finds its parallel in theological critical realism."[30] In Saether's opinion, attempts to match scientific critical realism with a corresponding theological critical realism seem parallel and consonant, but not connected.

The Danish philosopher Kees van Kooten Niekerk affirms the continuity between science and theology on a critical realist platform.[31] He suggests, despite the differences, theological inquiry presumes a critical realism that is quite similar to that presupposed in the sciences. Niekerk writes, "Science and theology in principle are justified in claiming that their statements and propositions tell something about a mind-independent reality."[32] He offers three reasons for the transferability of scientific critical realism to theology.[33] First, like science, theology makes cognitive claims; second, science seeks to explain sense-experience in terms of nature just as theology seeks to explain religious experience in terms of God. Third, both science and theology employ metaphors and models as approximate - not literal- descriptions of an external reality. Thus for Niekerk, the critical realism employed in science and in theology is parallel, consonant and connected.

---

30 Knut-Willy Saether, *Traces of God: Exploring John Polkinghorne on Theology and Science* (Trondheim, Norway: Tapir Academic Press, 2011), 54.

31 Peters and Peterson, "The Higgs Boson," 188. For details, refer to Kees van Kooten Niekerk, "A Critical Realist Perspective on the Dialogue between Theology and Science," in *Rethinking Theology and Science: Six Models for the Current Dialogue*, ed. Niels Henrik Gregersen and J. Wentzel van Huyssteen (Grand Rapids MI: William B. Eerdmans Publishing Co., 1998), 51-56.

32 Niekerk, "A Critical Realist Perspective," 78.

33 Ibid., 188. For details, refer to van Kooten Niekerk, "Critical Realism," in *Encyclopedia of Science and Religion,* ed. J. Wentzel Vrede van Huyssteen, vol. 1 (New York: Macmillan/Thomson Gale, 2003), 190-193.

Unlike Saether and Nierkerk, the British New Testament scholar Nicholas T. Wright proposes a unique form of critical realism for theology. Wright writes:

> This is a way of describing the process of knowing that acknowledges the reality of the thing known, as something other than the knower (hence "realism"), while fully acknowledging that the only access we have to this reality lies along the spiraling path of appropriate dialogue or conversation between the knower and the thing known (hence "critical").[34]

As seen above, there are different understandings of the use of critical realism in theology. Whether parallel, continuous, connected or unique, it is quite clear that critical realism has an intrinsic value both for science and theology.

Many scholars have contributed to the use of critical realism as a methodological bridge between science and theology, most remarkably Ian G. Barbour, Arthur Peacocke, John Polkinghorne, Wolfhart Pannenberg, Thomas Torrance, Sallie McFague, Philip Clayton, Wentzel van Huyssteen, Alister McGrath, Ernan McMullin, Robert John Russell, Ted Peters, and Nancey Murphy. The pioneering attempt to use critical realism as a methodological bridge between science and theology dates back to Ian G. Barbour's 1966 publication, *Issues in Science and Religion.* Barbour's critical realism holds that "the goal of science is to understand nature, not simply to control it or make predictions."[35] His critical realist view acknowledges "both the creativity of man's mind, and the existence of patterns in events that are not created by man's mind."[36] Like Barbour, Arthur Peacocke makes a significant contribution to the use of critical realism in science-theology dialogue. Peacocke asserts critical realism as the most reasonable epistemological

34 Nicholas T. Wright, *The New Testament and the People of God* (Minneapolis: Fortress Press, 1992), 35.

35 Barbour, *Issues in Science and Religion*, 138.

36 Ibid., 172.

choice, between the excesses of social constructivism and naïve realism, which responds to the need for "a defensible, non-naive scientific realism"[37] capable of being adequately informed by contemporary discoveries in physics. We shall be dealing in detail with the critical realist views of Barbour and Peacocke in the next chapter.

British theoretical physicist and theologian, John Polkinghorne, claims that the "critical realist quest for the best explanation provides a common ground on which the dialogue between science and theology can take place."[38] He asserts his critical realist claim:

> I believe that the advance of science is not just concerned with our ability to manipulate the physical world, but to gain knowledge of its actual nature. In a word, I am a realist. Of course, such knowledge is to a degree partial and corrigible. Our attainment is verisimilitude, not absolute truth. Our method is the creative interpretation of experience, not rigorous deduction from it. Thus I am a critical realist.[39]

According to Polkinghorne, "It is a critical realism that scientist-theologians defend. No naïve objectivity is involved in either discipline."[40] Polkinghorne's understanding of critical realism is based on the assumption that human rationality is able to understand a rational universe. He discusses:

---

37 Arthur Peacocke, *Intimations of Reality: Critical Realism in Science and Religion* (Notre Dame, IN: University of Notre Dame Press, 1984), 23.

38 John Polkinghorne, *Faith, Science, and Understanding* (New Haven, CT: Yale University Press, 2000), 203.

39 John Polkinghorne, *Belief in God in an Age of Science* (New Haven, CT: Yale University Press, 1998), 104.

40 John Polkinghorne, *Scientists as Theologians: A Comparison of the Writings of Ian G. Barbour, Arthur Peacocke and John Polkinghorne* (London: Society for Promoting Christian Knowledge, 1996), 14.

> Theologically this is to be understood as due to the universe's being a creation and we as creatures made in the image of the creator. The possibility of science is then the consequence of the deposit of the *imago dei* within humanity. The critical realism which I have been seeking to defend is thus found ... to be undergirded by a theological belief in the faithfulness of God, who has not created a world whose appearances will mislead the honest enquirer. The unity of knowledge is underwritten by the unity of the one true God; the veracity of well-motivated belief is underwritten by the reliability of God.[41]

While differentiating between the disciplines of science and theology, Polkinghorne explains how scientists and theologians have adopted a critical realism and use it as a methodological choice in bridging the two disciplines.

Scottish Protestant Theologian Thomas F. Torrance is one of the most rigorous exponents of a critical realist approach to issues in science and theology. He has treated theology as an objective inquiry and has clearly identified the interconnection between the knower and the known.[42] Wentzel van Huyssteen, Professor of Theology and Science at Princeton Theological Seminary, introduces a 'weak' version of critical realism in theology. He states, "A qualified or weak form of critical realism, therefore, does not at all offer a strong defense of theism, but attempts to deal with and make more plausible the cognitive claims of religious language and theological reflection."[43] Van Huyssteen views critical realism not as an established theory of explanation, rather as a promising and suggestive hypothesis. While affirming the provisionality of models, van Huyssteen shows the similarity between the epistemic

41 Polkinghorne, *Belief in God in an Age of Science,* 122.

42 See Thomas F. Torrance, *Belief in Science and in Christian Life: The Relevance of Michel Polanyi's Thought for Christian Faith and Life* (Edinburgh: Handsel Press, 1980).

43 J. Wentzel van Huyssteen, *Essays in Postfoundationalist Theology* (Grand Rapids, MI: William B. Eerdmans Publishing Co., 1997), 43.

enterprises of science and theology and how the critical realist approach can be adopted both in science and theology:

> For this approach in which scientist and therefore also the theologian attempts to say something about a reality beyond our language, by means of provisional tentative models, in terms of human constructs, the term critical realism might be fruitful. A critical-realist approach to theology now becomes feasible because metaphors and models play such a decisive role in all cognitive development- also in theology. A critical realist stand is realistic because in the process of theological theorizing this concept enables us to recognize the cognitive and referential nature of analogical language as a form of indirect speech. It is also critical, however, because, the role of metaphorical language in theology would teach us that models should never be absolutized or ideologized, but should retain their openness and provisionality throughout the process of theorizing.[44]

Focusing on the significance of "metaphor" as a stimulus to theological conceptualizing, van Huyssteen offers a critical realist perspective on the nature and rationality of theological statements and doctrines. American feminist theologian Sallie McFague's metaphorical theology can be viewed almost directly in van Huyssteen's vein. Drawing insights from the works of Ian G. Barbour (similarities between metaphors and models in theology and science) and Paul Ricoeur (epistemic tension between simile and dissimile), McFague develops a metaphorical theology offering new insights into ecology and theology.[45]

44 J. Wentzel van Huyssteen, *Theology and the Justification of Faith: Constructing Theories in Systematic Theology* (Grand Rapids, MI: William B. Eerdmans, 1989), 142.

45 Sallie McFague, *Metaphorical Theology: Models of God in Religious Language* (Philadelphia: Fortress Press, 1982), 225.

British Irish theologian Alister McGrath provides an integrationist worldview of critical realism in *A Scientific Theology* by viewing theology as a discipline that can benefit from the methodologies of the natural sciences and by freeing theology from intellectual isolationism.[46] McGrath critiques the domination of apologetic concerns in the use of critical realism in theology and tries to legitimize the use of it by insisting on the *a posteriori* nature of a scientific theology:

> A scientific theology conceives the theological enterprise as a principled attempt to give an account of the reality of God ... Declining to make *a priori* prejudgments concerning what might be known of God, and the manner in which that knowledge should be established, a scientific theology approaches such questions in the light of what is actually known about God. A scientific theology conceives itself as an *a posteriori* discipline, responding to and offering an account of what may be known of God through revelation, taking full account of the stratified nature of that knowledge of God.[47]

McGrath critiques the scientist-theologians' use of critical realism as distanced from the main-line academic community. Unlike many other scientist-theologians, McGrath attempts to retrieve the original meaning of critical realism by borrowing concepts like *a priori* and *a posteriori* from the philosophy of science, especially from Roy Bhaskar. For McGrath, God is epistemologically known *a posteriori* and ontologically existent *a priori*. The object of knowledge (ontology) should determine the conditions under which one can obtain knowledge (epistemology). McGrath further explains:

---

46 McGrath claims that theology has developed an intellectual insularity by way of detaching from the debates and resources of the mainline academic community. Alister McGrath, *A Scientific Theology: Reality*, vol. 2 of *A Scientific Theology* (Grand Rapids, MI: William. B. Eerdmans Publishing Co., 2002), 208.

47 McGrath, *A Scientific Theology*, xi.

> A fundamental assumption of a scientific theology is that, since the ontology of the natural world is determined by and reflects its status as God's creation, the working methods and assumptions of those natural sciences which engage most directly with that natural world are of direct relevance to the working methods and assumptions of a responsible Christian theology.[48]

According to McGrath, the critical realist approach is "both intellectually habitable and theologically responsible."[49] He uses the concept of creation, as quoted above, to prove his claim that the method of natural sciences has direct relevance to the method of theology.

German theologian Wolfhart Pannenberg develops the concept of contingency to make sense of critical realism in science-theology dialogue with reference to the dependence of the finite world on God. According to Pannenberg, "Any contemporary discussion between theology and science should focus in the first place on the question of what modern science and especially what modern physics can say about the contingency of the world as a whole and of every part in it."[50] Pannenberg asserts that "the existence of world as a whole and of all its parts is contingent. The existence of the whole world is contingent in the sense that it need not be at all. It owes its existence to the free activity of divine creation. So does every single part of the world."[51] Exploring the philosophical meaning of contingency both in the philosophy of science as well as in creation theology, Pannenberg makes a clear connection between science and theology.

American philosopher of science Ernan McMullin, introduces the idea of "consonance" between theology and science in

---

48 McGrath, *A Scientific Theology*, 245.

49 Ibid., 315.

50 Wolfhart Pannenberg, "The Doctrine of Creation and Modern Science," *Zygon: Journal of Religion and Science*, vol. 23, no. 1 (March, 1998): 12. For details, refer to p. 3-21.

51 Ibid., 9.

the context of the relation between Big Bang cosmology and the doctrine of creation *ex nihilo*. He presents consonance as a coherent worldview to which all forms of human knowing contribute, including science and theology, while at the same time calculating a "constant slight shift" in the worldview.[52] The American systematic theologian Ted Peters develops the concept of consonance into "Hypothetical Consonance."[53] Peters advocates a consonance in the weak sense rather than in the strong sense, as we have not yet found complete harmony.

Philip Clayton, another American philosopher theologian, also incorporates the Lakatosian methodology into his theological thinking. According to Clayton, in the natural sciences "explanation" is the interpretation of physical data.[54] In the social sciences, explanation means understanding as one interprets both physical data as well as the experience of the actor-subjects, while in theology, explanations are validated through inter-subjective testability by the religious community. Clayton draws insights from Lakatos' requirement that competing explanatory hypotheses

---

52 For details, refer to Ernan McMullin, "How Should Cosmology Relate to Theology?" in *The Sciences and Technology in the Twentieth Century*, ed. Arthur R. Peacocke (Notre Dame, IN: University of Notre Dame Press, 1981), 17-57.

53 See Ted Peters, "On Creating the Cosmos," in *Physics, Philosophy and Theology: A Common Quest for Understanding*, ed. Robert John Russell, William R. Stoeger, S.J. and George V. Coyne, S.J. (Vatican: Vatican Observatory Publications, 1988), 274-276. The scientist theologian Robert John Russell also develops the idea of consonance and dissonance as an important methodological step, especially while bridging between science and theology with specific reference to Big Bang cosmology and creation theology. Taking into account the various models of Big Bang cosmology Russell claims, "If dissonance is treated in a positive way it might lead to new insights and an even deeper consonance. Moreover, by recognizing that what might be seen as consonant or as dissonant can change in time, we can build change directly into the relation between science and theology." Robert John Russell, *Cosmology: From Alpha to Omega* (Minneapolis: Fortress Press, 2008), 12. For details, refer to, 11-14.

54 Philip Clayton, *Explanation from Physics to Theology: An Essay in Rationality and Religion* (New Haven, CT: Yale University Press, 1989).

can be assessed by a previously specified set of criteria held by the community.

American philosopher of science and theologian, Nancey Murphy, provides a postmodern epistemology for critical realism by adopting Imre Lakatos' methodology in her *Theology in the Age of Scientific Reasoning.*[55] Murphy makes a crucial modification of Lakatos's understanding of "novel facts" in a scientific research program and extends it beyond the natural sciences to provide a scientific status for theology.

Drawing insights from Barbour (analogical methodology), Peacocke (epistemic hierarchy), and Murphy (Lakotosian theological research programs), the scientist theologian, Robert John Russell, introduces the method of Creative Mutual Interaction (CMI) to integrate method in science and method in theology. Russell's approach is also informed by the work of theologian Wolfhart Pannenberg.[56] Russell suggests eight distinct paths between science and theology. The basic building blocks of CMI are the hermeneutical circles internal to science and theology, which represent Barbour's theory of critical realism. These circles are embedded within Arthur Peacocke's hierarchy of the sciences and then connected via the five upward and three downward paths.

---

55 Nancey Murphy, *Theology in the Age of Scientific Reasoning* (Ithaca, NY: Cornell University Press, 1990).

56 Russell explores the multiple meanings of contingency (contingency of the world as a whole and of its parts) through a typology to analyze the meaning of contingency in the writings of Wolfhart Pannenberg. Russell, *Cosmology,* 14-15. Pannenberg's ideas of contingency can be seen in Wolfhart Pannenberg, "The Doctrine of Creation and Modern Science," in *Cosmos as Creation: Theology and Science in Consonance*, ed. Ted Peters (Nashville: Abingdon Press, 1989), 152-76, 288; Robert John Russell, "Contingency in Physics and Cosmology: A Critique of the Theology of Wolfhart Pannenberg," *Zygon: Journal of Religion and Science,* vol. 23, no. 1 (1998): 23-43.

The five paths which move upwards from science to theology represents the role of theology in critically appropriating the discoveries of science.[57] The three paths which move downwards from theology to science represent how theology can indirectly influence science.[58] Thus using CMI, Russell tries to integrate method in science and method in theology.

---

57 Path 1: Theories in physics can act directly as data which places constraints over theology. So, for example, a theological theory about divine action should not violate special relativity theory. Path 2: Theories can act directly as data either to be "explained" by theology or as a basis for a theological constructive argument. Thus, t=0 in standard Big Bang was often explained theologically via creation *ex nihilo*. Path 3: Theories in physics, after philosophical analysis, can act indirectly as data for theology. For example, an indeterministic interpretation of quantum mechanics can function within philosophical theology as making intelligible the idea of non-interventionist objective divine action. Path 4: Theories in physics can also act indirectly as the data for theology when they are incorporated into a fully-articulated philosophy of nature (for example, that of Alfred North Whitehead). Finally, path 5: Theories in physics can function heuristically in the theological context of discovery, by providing conceptual or aesthetic inspiration, and so on. So biological evolution may inspire a sense of God's immanence in nature. Russell, *Cosmology,* 303.

58 In path 6, Russell claims that historically, theological ideas have provided some of the philosophical assumptions which underlie scientific methodology. In Russell's view, historians and philosophers of science have shown in detail how the doctrine of creation *ex nihilo* played an important role in the rise of modern science by combining the Greek assumption of the rationality of the world and the theological assumption of the contingency of the world. Russell further claims that these helped give birth to the empirical method and the use of mathematics to represent natural processes. In path 7, Russell argues that theological theories can act as sources of inspiration in the scientific "context of discovery," which means, theological theories may play a heuristic role in the development of scientific models as well as in the construction of new scientific theories. Russell makes reference to the example of the subtle influence of atheism on Fred Hoyle's search for a steady state cosmology. In path 8, Russell claims that theological theories can provide criteria for choosing between rival scientific theories. He says, "If one considers a theological theory as true, then one can delineate what conditions must obtain within physics for the possibility of its being true. These conditions in turn can serve as motivations for an individual research scientist or group of colleagues to choose to pursue a particular scientific theory. Ibid., 305.

The above descriptions reveal how scientist theologians use critical realism as a methodological bridge between science and theology. According to Russell:

> Critical realism has continued to be defended, deployed and diversified widely in theology and science, and it continues to be presupposed both by most working scientists and by many theologians, and in much of the public discourse about both science and religion. On balance I believe it to be of enduring importance, both for its crucial role in the historical developments of the past decades and as a point of departure for future research.[59]

Barbour's explanation of models and theories, Peacocke's emergent holism, Polkinghorne's understanding of the God-world relationship, Pannenberg's treatment of contingency, Torrance's explanation of the knower-known relatonship, Sallie McFague's metaphorical theology, Alister McGrath's scientific theology, Wentzel van Huyssteen's affirmation of the provisionality of models and metaphors, Ernan McMullin's idea of consonance, Ted Peters' hypothetical consonance, Philip Clayton's understanding of "explanation," Nancey Murphy's theological research program, and Robert John Russell's creative mutual interaction are evidence to the fact that critical realism is being widely used in science-theology dialogue.

## Conclusion

In this chapter, I focused mainly on critical realism as used in science-theology dialogue. The chapter began with a brief historical overview of critical realism based on the views of British philosopher, Roy Bhaskar, and concluded by portraying the wide use of critical realism in science-theology dialogue. At the end of this chapter, two things strike me: science requires some extra-scientific reality in order to be science and critical realism

59 Russell, *Cosmology*, 9.

has an intrinsic value both for science and theology. In spite of the various attempts to explain critical realism, epistemological concerns emerge in diverse modes and remain vague and complex while bridging science and theology. So we ask the question: what is fundamentally critical about critical realism in science-theology dialogue?

# 2. What is Critical about Critical Realism in Science - Theology Dialogue?

Scientist theologians, in general, believe that critical realism is a valid theory of knowledge both in science and theology. Most of them agree that theology almost shares with science the same form of rationality and that the epistemic project of the two disciplines is one and the same: the exploration of reality. Many argue that the best construction of theological theories is to be formed by epistemological standards and methods borrowed from or, modeled upon, contemporary science and philosophy of science. Hence, criteria for good theology are developed by examining the criteria for good science. The basic purpose of these authors is to find resonance between science and theology through the mutual embracing of critical realism. Do theologians borrow too liberally and profusely from scientific data to suit their theological purposes? For example, Barbour develops his critical realism in relation to religion from its usual locus in science. Peacocke develops his critical realism depending on a biologically oriented theological anthropology. Polkinghorne develops his ideas based on his claim that faith is reasonable.

Critical realism is a philosophical framework that enhances the dialogue between natural sciences and theology by accounting for epistemological and ontological elements of scientific thinking.

Then the emerging question in science-theology dialogue is whether a single position on knowledge like critical realism can effectively connect both disciplines because of the contingencies that characterize each discipline? It is presupposed that both science and theology hold a common position on the nature of knowledge. But do they adequately account for God as a distinct object of theoretical knowledge?

Critical realism is employed in science to explain how we come to know the existence of an extra-scientific reality from empirical data. When such a critical realism is adapted to theology, its epistemological value is warranted only by an *a priori* ontological belief in the existence of God. In other words, the cognitive claims in theology are valid only if we assume the existence of a divine reality. But in the original work of Roy Bhaskar, his most fundamental commitment to realism is capable of making sense of everyday perception and scientific experimentation without invoking extra-natural powers. Bhaskar writes, "The aim of science is the production of the knowledge of the mechanisms of the production of phenomena in nature that combine to generate the actual flux of phenomena of the world.These mechanisms, which are the intransitive object of scientific enquiry, endure and act quite independently of men."[60] It is quite clear that all that Bhaskar needs is the existence of some "enduring and transfactually active mechanisms,"[61] capable of explaining the experimental success of science, not a transcendental divine intellect. On the contrary, critical realism with regard to theological statements is fundamentally linked with the belief in God. From that point of view, the domination of apologetic concerns in theology to face the explanatory power of natural sciences as well as to represent theology as a monarch over the natural sciences is an epistemological concern. How to justify the apologetic interest of scientist-theologians in defending the epistemic freedom and privilege of the theological endeavour against that of the natural

60 Bhaskar, *A Realist Theory of Science*, 17.

61 Ibid., 20.

sciences? All these concerns call for a detailed inquiry into the use of critical realism in science-theology dialogue. In response, I will delineate the critical realist views of Ian G. Barbour, Arthur Peacocke and Nancey Murphy as they represent significant phases in the development of the use of critical realism in the conversation between science and theology.

## 2.1 Critical Realism in Science-Theology Dialogue: Barbour and Peacocke

Ian G. Barbour, in his 1966 publication, *Issues in Science and Religion* provides a foundational definition of critical realism:

> Critical realism acknowledges the indirectness of reference and the realistic intent of language as used in the scientific community. It can point to both the extraordinarily abstract character of theoretical physics and the necessity of experimental observation which distinguishes it from pure mathematics. It recognizes that no theory is an exact description of the world, and the world is such as to bear interpretation in some ways and not in others. It affirms the role of mental construction and imaginative activity in the formation of theories, and it asserts that some constructs agree with observations better than others only because events have an objective pattern.[62]

Barbour introduces critical realism as one of the best epistemic stances for scientists to uphold, given the shortcomings of positivism (theory as summary of empirical data), instrumentalism (theory as useful tool for control and prediction), idealism (theory as mental structure) and naïve realism (theory as representation of the world).[63] Barbour argues, "If the goal of science is to understand nature, we can unify the concern of empirical testing found in positivism with the concern for intellectual coherence found in

62 Barbour, *Issues in Science and Religion*, 172.

63 Ibid., 138.

idealism, while avoiding the exclusive preoccupation of either."[64] He further affirms this position in *Religion and Science*: "Against instrumentalism, which sees both scientific theories and religious beliefs as human constructs as useful for specific human purposes, I advocate a critical realism holding that both communities make cognitive claims about realities beyond the human world."[65]

Barbour introduces four different models for relating science and religion: conflict, independence, dialogue and integration.[66] Conflict refers to the image of warfare between science and religion. Scientific materialism and biblical literalism are seen in this light. Independence is a way of looking at the two enterprises as totally independent and autonomous, thereby avoiding conflicts between the two. This view focuses mainly on the contrasting methods and different languages of the two disciplines. The dialogue model takes into account limit questions (boundary conditions) in the respective disciplines, methodological parallels in scientific and theological reasoning, and nature-centered spirituality. In the integration model, Barbour finds three distinct versions: natural theology, theology of nature and systematic synthesis.[67]

Barbour proposes four criteria for assessing theories in normal scientific research: Agreement with data, coherence (consistency with other accepted theories), scope (applicability to wide ranges) and fertility (current ability and future promise for research).[68] Considering the three main western theories of truth

64 Barbour, *Issues in Science and Religion*, 172-73.

65 Ian G. Barbour, *Religion and Science: Historical and Contemporary Issues* (San Francisco: Harper, 1997), 89.

66 Barbour, *Religion and Science*, 77.

67 Natural theology claims that the existence of God can be inferred from the evidences of design in nature, of which science has made us more aware. In a theology of nature, the main sources of theology lie outside science, but scientific theories may affect the reformulation of certain doctrines, particularly the doctrines of creation and human nature. In systematic synthesis, both science and religion contribute to the development of an inclusive metaphysics, such as that of process philosophy. Ibid., 98.

68 Ibid., 109.

(correspondence, coherence and pragmatic theories), Barbour articulates his critical realist view:

> My conclusion is that the meaning of truth is correspondence with reality. But because reality is inaccessible to us, the criteria of truth must include all four of the criteria mentioned above. The criteria taken together include the valid insights in all these views of truth. One or another of the criteria may be more important than the others at a particular stage of scientific inquiry. Because correspondence is taken as the definition of truth, this is a form of realism, but it is a critical realism because a combination of criteria is used.[69]

Barbour's primary purpose is to clear the ground for a science-theology dialogue by arguing for anti-reductionism in all its forms, deploying an overlap between scientific and theological language through the common use of metaphors and models, developing a critical realist view of both science and religion/theology, and exhibiting an analogical relationship between scientific and theological reasoning. He summarizes his views as follows:

> Models and theories are abstract symbol systems which inadequately and selectively represent particular aspects of the world for specific purposes. This view preserves the scientist's realistic intent while recognizing that models and theories are imaginative human constructs. Models, on this reading, are to be taken seriously but not literally; they are neither literal pictures [naïve realism] nor useful fictions [instrumentalism] but limited and inadequate ways of imagining what is not observable. They make tentative ontological claims that there are entities in the world something like those postulated in the models.[70]

69 Ibid., 110.

70 Ian G. Barbour, *Religion in an Age of Science,* Gifford Lectures 1989-1991, vol. 1 (New York: Harper, 1990), 43. The same can also be seen in Barbour,

Barbour tries to employ critical realism in theological matters on the basis of the use of critical realism in science. Perhaps the most characteristic feature of Barbour's critical realism is his position that structural parallels exist between science and religion. Barbour believes that they share similar epistemological structures. He demonstrates the use of metaphors and models within the context of community dependent paradigms both in scientific and theological practices. Barbour claims that our access to reality is mediated by concepts and theories. Consequently, the data is theory laden, and *vice versa*. As a result, science and theology work through similar hermeneutical circles of reasoning and therefore exhibit methodological parallels.[71] The scientist uses his/her creativity and imagination to develop analogies and models which provide the basis for the formulation of theory as well as the link between data and theory. The newly formulated theory, in turn, influences the interpretation of the experimental data and is subject to criticism by the paradigm community. The interdependence of theory and data is significant in Barbour's account of the structure of scientific reasoning. The critical nature of realism results from the analogies and models used.

The structure of theological reasoning is analogous to that of science. Instead of experimental data in science, the "data" in religion consists of religious experience, story, myth and ritual.[72] As with the inductive ascent in science, the theologian uses creative imagination and tradition to develop analogies and models to derive a theory that integrates the religious data.[73] As with the deductive descent in science, the theory in theology is tested against religious data, where the data is necessarily theory laden because the theory influences the religious experience. Religious reasoning, like scientific reasoning, takes the form of a

---

*Religion and Science*, 117.

71 Barbour, *Religion in an Age of Science*, 111, 117.

72 Ibid., 113-114.

73 Ibid., 36.

hermeneutical circle. Here also, the critical nature of the realism results from the analogies and models employed.

While drawing similarity between the structures of scientific and religious reasoning, Barbour shows that they differ at several crucial points.[74] In spite of the differences, Barbour finds common functions and attitudes to underpin the structural parallels:

> Science is neither as objective, nor religion as subjective, as these two opposing schools of thought [positivism and existentialism] both assumed. Despite the presence of distinctive functions and attitudes in religion which have no parallels in science, there are also functions and attitudes in common wherein I see differences of degree rather than absolute dichotomy.[75]

Barbour's use of critical realism is based on a Hempelian hypothetico-deductive method. It incorporates a form of Popperian falsificationism placed within a Kuhnian framework which is both contextualist and historicist. It further provides a metaphysical ground of unity incorporating a Whiteheadian metaphysics by stressing the interconnected web of reality.[76] Critical realism, for Barbour, provides a holistic, unified and a complementary worldview. It introduces the possibility of methodological unity and cohesion in scientific and theological

---

74 Science, in general, deals with matter, and analogies are used to explain empirical reality whereas, religion deals with a non-empirical reality (God). Barbour notes important differences in the "data" of religion (story, myth and rituals, etc.) compared to that of science (experimental data). Religious models serve non-cognitive and affective functions which are missing in science, such as eliciting attitudes, personal involvement, and transformation. In science, theories tend to dominate models, while in religion, models are more influential than theories. Religion lacks lower level laws such as those found in science. Religion is rich with elements such as story, ritual, myth and revelation which are rarely found in science. Ibid., 110.

75 Ian G. Barbour, *Myths, Models, and Paradigms: A Comparative Study in Science and Religion* (San Francisco: Harper & Row, 1974), 5-6.

76 Russell, *Cosmology*, 5.

reasoning. In other words, the adoption of critical realism allows Barbour to reject an absolute dichotomy between subjective and objective knowledge and therefore to argue for a deep similarity between science and theology.

Like Barbour, Arthur Peacocke finds critical realism an adequate epistemological choice for dialogue between science and theology.[77] According to Peacocke, "Critical realism recognizes that it is still only the aim of science to depict reality and that this allows gradations in acceptance of the 'truth' of scientific theories. It is a critical realism about entities, structures and processes which figure in scientific theories (the 'terms' of the theories) rather than about theories as such."[78] Peacocke spells out his understanding of critical realism in *Intimations of Reality:*

> In practice, working scientists, I would argue, adopt a skeptical and qualified critical realism, according to which their theories and models are proposed and regarded as "candidates for reality." Scientists aim to depict previously hidden or unknown structures and processes of the real world, and the terms in their theories and the features of their models are intended genuinely to refer to a real world. They have no illusions, however, about the performance of their proposals and the massive qualifications required of any attribution of "truth" to them.[79]

Assuming that scientific theory is the scientific correlative of theological doctrine, Peacocke draws comparisons between the two enterprises and thus classifies:

> "naïve realism," as theological fundamentalism about received doctrines; "positivism," as biblical literalism

77 Arthur Peacocke, *Theology for a Scientific Age: Being and Becoming-Natural, Divine and Human* (Minneapolis: Fortress Press, 1993), 217.

78 Peacocke, *Theology for a Scientific Age,* 12.

79 Arthur Peacocke, *Intimations of Reality: Critical Realism in Science and Religion* (Notre Dame, IN: University of Notre Dame Press, 1984), 25.

> (reliance on biblical texts as empirical data and disregard for interpretative categories); "instrumentalism," whereby religious myths and stories are either simple aids to the pursuit of policies of life by capturing the imagination and strengthening the mind, or are able to evoke mystical experiences; and "critical realism," whereby theological concepts and models are partial and inadequate but necessary and, indeed, the only ways of referring to the *reality* that is God and God's relation to humanity.[80]

Peacocke introduces the concept of epistemic emergence among disciplines. He presents a series of emergent levels both vertically and horizontally comprising the disciplines of the natural sciences, human sciences and theology.[81] Along the vertical axis, the lower levels place constraints over the upper levels while the upper levels are emergent and cannot be reduced to lower levels. In complex systems, emergent order results from the non-linear dynamics of systems whose various components exhibit a strong internal bonding. Due to internal interaction, system-wide behavior occurs which is irreducible to the bottom-up causality of the parts, and which becomes a distinct higher level reality exerting whole-part causality on the parts themselves.[82] In living systems, "changes at the micro-level, that of the constituent of the constituent units, are what they are because of their incorporation into the system as a whole, which is exerting specific constraints on its units, making them behave otherwise than they would in isolation."[83] For instance, due to whole-part causality, chemical

80 Peacocke, *Intimations of Reality*, 40.

81 Peacocke, *Theology for a Scientific Age*, 217.

82 Peacocke routinely conflates top-down and whole-part causality. He really means the latter. The goal of demonstrating genuine top-down causality has still not been achieved. Peacocke's whole-part and bottom-up causal processes act as two different natural causal vectors, giving theology a specific explanatory function concerning the action of God. The role of whole-part causation in no way derogates from that of bottom-up causation. Ibid., 54.

83 Peacocke, *Theology for a Scientific Age*, 53-54.

reactions behave differently in living organisms than they do in a test tube. Moreover, since these whole-part influences have their own integrity, reality stratifies into distinct, irreducible levels (physical, biological, psychological, and cultural). The horizontal axis of the diagram ranks natural phenomena in terms of their increasing size within the same epistemic level.

However, Peacocke warns of a danger hidden in the whole-part, bottom-up approaches. For Peacocke, the description of this two-way process as 'reductionism' is misleading.[84] He distinguishes two types of reductionism. While using methodological reductionism, he cautions against the pitfalls of ontological reductionism. Reductionism, Peacocke explains, cannot do justice to the emergent phenomena and properties which manifest at different levels of complexity, making it impossible to describe such phenomena adequately within a reductionist framework. Moreover, Peacocke argues that to discard reductionism authorizes us to attribute reality to a wider range of entities than a physicalist reductionism allows for. He says, "The entities to which the 'theories and experimental laws' refer in our epistemological analyses, correspond, however inadequately and provisionally, to realities which must be deemed to exist at the various levels being studied--that is, they also have an ontological reference, however elusive."[85]

According to Peacocke, theology enjoys an epistemic primacy over all other disciplines, as the theological enterprise encompasses humans, the world and God. Theology, Peacocke argues, is the intellectual analysis of the characteristic human activity which is the "exercise of religion."[86] This exercise operates at "a level in the hierarchy of complexity that is more intricate than any of the levels studied by the individual, natural, social, and other human sciences."[87] The theological enterprise is in fact a reflection which encompasses humans, the world and God by

84 Ibid., 54.

85 Ibid.

86 Ibid., 36.

87 Ibid.

standing at the summit of conceivable complexity and wholeness, and theologians are allowed to ask (rhetorically) whether "perhaps theology, if no longer medieval 'queen of the sciences,' may at least be accorded the honors of a constitutional monarch."[88] In addition to the epistemological primacy of theology, Peacocke asserts the ontological primacy of theology over other disciplines.

Both Barbour and Peacocke are convinced of the effectiveness of critical realism in fostering science-theology dialogue. Both of them assert the roles of metaphor and analogy in achieving knowledge, especially in theology. Like Barbour, who opts for a metaphysical approach that is indebted to process thought, Peacocke opts for a philosophical tradition in panentheism, a belief system which holds the view that the divine interpenetrates every part of nature. In sum, he emphasizes the emergence of human personhood as a significant feature in the unfolding of life, views nature as a hierarchy of communicating levels, and describes the theological significance of the God-world relationship.

Barbour and Peacocke see critical realism as a position that sustains scientific and theological claims better than other positions. However, their approaches do raise concerns. For example, Peacocke tries to establish a connection between critical realism and the God-world panentheistic model, as Barbour does between critical realism and process thought. While Peacocke's emergence theory may well account for the stratification of distinct levels within creation, it cannot account for the reality of God within a theistic (as opposed to pantheistic) understanding. While the epistemological relation between higher and lower levels may remain uniform up through the theological level, there is an ontological rupture since God Himself is not an emergent reality. Does theologically oriented critical realism result in confusion between the epistemic project of the natural sciences and the discipline of theology? A better account for critical realism is required for interfacing science and theology within an interdisciplinary context. To this end, in the next section, I explain

88 Ibid., 37.

in details Nancey Murphy's understanding of critical realism in the science-theology dialogue.

## 2.2 Critical Realism in Science Theology Dialogue: Nancey Murphy

Nancey Murphy critiques Barbour's and Peacocke's espousal of critical realism as modern, and poses postmodern challenges to the modern understanding of critical realism. She argues that "critical realism is a doctrine at home only in a modern worldview."[89] Murphy characterizes modern thought as dominated by three central philosophical theses: epistemological foundationalism, a representational-expressivity theory of language, and individualism.[90] Epistemological foundationalism is the view that knowledge can only be justified by finding indubitable foundational beliefs upon which to construct the rest of knowledge. The representational-expressivist theory of language is the view that language must gain its primary meaning by representing the objects or facts to which it refers; otherwise it merely expresses the attitudes of the speaker. Individualism is an approach to ethics and political philosophy which views the individual as prior to community, and community as merely a collection of like individuals. Thus, modern thought defines a three dimensional space (epistemological, linguistic and metaphysical) within a Cartesian coordinate system in which modern thinkers can be located.[91] Murphy writes:

> Modern scientific realists disagree among themselves about their exact location in the upper-right-hand quadrant, distancing themselves from the extreme representationalist position of the "naïve realists" but never clear about

89 Murphy, "Bridging Theology and Science in a Postmodern Age," in *Bridging Science and Religion,* ed. Ted Peters and Gayman Bennett (Minneapolis: Fortress Press, 2003), 35.

90 Murphy, "Bridging Theology and Science in a Postmodern Age," 36.

91 Nancey Murphy, *Anglo-American Postmodernity: Philosophical Perspectives on Science, Religion, and Ethics* (Colorado: Westview Press, 1997), 40.

> *how far* they are from the naïve realists. I suspect that this ambiguity concerning exactly *how* representative scientific language is supposed to be what allows critical realists to avoid the horns of a dilemma: if no claims are made for representation--if it is never specified in what sense knowledge corresponds to reality--then the position is safe from all criticisms of correspondence theories of truth and of representational theories of language, but it is vacuous. But if one does claim to know how the sentence, model, or theory does and does not correspond with reality, one runs into all the same problems that confronts the naïve realist. Modern opponents of the scientific realists can be positioned in the lower-left-hand quadrant. (All are atomists rather than idealists, so we can ignore the *z* axis).[92]

In contrast to the modern understanding of critical realism, Murphy offers a postmodern explanation of critical realism. To accomplish this, she utilizes two important postmodern philosophical positions: epistemological holism and the theory of meaning as used in philosophy of language.[93] Murphy substantiates her thought by relying on W.V. Quine's view of knowledge. According to Quine, modern empiricism is conditioned mainly by two dogmas: "One is a belief in some fundamental cleavage between truths which are *analytic*, or grounded in meanings independently of matters of fact, and truths which are *synthetic*, or grounded in fact. The other dogma is *reductionism*: the belief that each meaningful statement is equivalent to some logical constructs upon terms which refer to immediate experience."[94]

Quine argues that both dogmas are ill founded and instead suggests that knowledge is a construct in which changes are made

92 Ibid., 40-41.

93 Ibid., 39.

94 Willard V.O. Quine, "Two Dogmas of Empiricism," *Philosophical Review,* 40 (1951): 20. For details, see p. 20-43.

on the basis of pragmatic considerations.[95] For him, total science is like a force field whose boundary conditions are experience and pragmatic considerations. Murphy traces a similar thought in Karl Popper's philosophy of science. According to Popper, factual statements are provisionally accepted, but if questioned can be subjected to test, driven deeper. The scientific community decides which facts are to be considered solid; thus an element of conventionalism enters science even at its most basic level.[96] Murphy spots a much more radical thought in Thomas Kuhn, who argued for the theory dependence and community dependence of facts, claiming that the very meaning of terms in a factual statement is a function of theoretical assumptions. Kuhn's view is holistic in that a paradigm is accepted or rejected as a whole.[97]

Murphy's emphasis on the representational-expressivist theory of language is rooted in Ludwig Wittgenstein's *Philosophical Investigations*.[98] For Wittgenstein, languages are "forms of life." To study language is to examine the "language games" in which the speakers participate.[99] Language does not relate to the world in one particular way; nor can the conditions of the meaningfulness of an utterance be accounted for, except to say that the meaning will be found in the use. Moreover, he showed that there could be no language that merely expresses private sensations.[100] For him, language must be public from the very start or it is not language at all. According to Murphy, a non-individualist or corporate view of community is built into holist epistemology and the postmodern understanding of the language. Thus, language and the search for

95 Quine, "Two Dogmas of Empiricism," 20-23.

96 Karl Popper, *The Logic of Scientific Discovery* (New York: Routledge, 1977).

97 Thomas Kuhn, *The Structure of Scientific Revolutions*, 2nd edition (Chicago: The University of Chicago Press), 1987.

98 Ludwig Wittgenstein, *Philosophical Investigations,* trans. G.E.M. Anscombe (New York: The MacMillan Company, 1953).

99 Wittgenstein, *Philosophical Investigations,* 33e-34e, 167e.

100 Ibid., 189e.

knowledge are practices, dependent upon tradition, which are communal achievements.

Based on the strong program in the sociology of science developed by David Bloor, Barry Barnes, and others, Murphy shows critical realists' association with modern thought.[101] The strong program considers all human knowledge to be shaped by some social component in its formation process. Bloor regards all products of science as social constructions.[102] In a strong program, a "sociologist is concerned with knowledge, including scientific knowledge, purely as a natural phenomenon."[103] In Bloor's view, all scientific theories are influenced by social factors, beliefs, cultural context and self-interest. His research shows the influence of sociological forces on the decisions scientists make when rearranging their web of beliefs.

Aware of the sociological accounts Murphy critiques, critical realists regard their own position as a middle way between naïve realism (scientific theories are not calculating devices but rather literal expressions of unobservable aspects of the real world) and sociological accounts.[104] The debate between critical realists and sociologists is confusing because critical realists accept the same facts about science as the sociologists: "the under-determination of theory by data; the theory-ladenness of data; the effect on perception of prior belief; the influence in theory construction of ideals of natural order; of tacit assumptions embedded in paradigms; the shift in conceptual frameworks from one era to another."[105] However, when sociologists demonstrate by means of historical examples the value of sociological factors for explaining

101 For details, see David Bloor, *Knowledge and Social Imagery*, 2nd edition (Chicago: The University of Chicago Press, 1991). Also see David Bloor, *Knowledge and Social Imagery*, 2nd edition (Chicago: The University of Chicago Press, 1991); Barry Barnes, *Interests and the Growth of Knowledge* (London: Routledge, 1977).

102 Bloor, *Knowledge and Social Imagery*, 5.

103 Ibid.

104 Murphy, "Bridging Theology and Science in a Postmodern Age," 42.

105 Murphy, *Anglo-American Postmodernity*, 43.

the decisions scientists make within the area permitted by rational constraints, critical realists reject this sociological move. So, Murphy argues that the critical realist position remains strictly modern:

> It is governed by the metaphor of knowledge as a picture or representation of reality. Yet unlike naïve realism, it does not occupy the extreme foundationalist position on the epistemological axis, but rather has moved some distance toward skepticism in response to the historians' and sociologists' accounts of the underdetermination and changeability of scientific knowledge. Likewise critical realists have pulled back from the extreme representational position on the linguistic axis; they highlight the metaphorical nature of the scientific language; they see scientific models not as literal pictures of reality but as partial, tentative representations of what there is.[106]

Proponents of the strong program entirely reject the modern representational view of knowledge. Murphy writes, "Confusion enters the discussion when critical realists interpret sociologists' positions in terms of their own modern axes--because the sociologists do not hold the foundationalist-representational view of knowledge and language they place them in the skeptical–expressivist quadrant of modern conceptual place."[107] Murphy further rules out the claim that critical realism is a middle position between naïve realism and the sociologists' position as there can be no midpoint between positions that are not located in the same space.

Murphy warns that "the association of critical realism with modern thought warrants a practical caution. Conceptual changes once begun seldom (if ever) reverse. Therefore, it may be wise to use a postmodern basis for dialogue between science

106 Murphy, "Bridging Theology and Science in a Postmodern Age," 44.

107 Ibid.

and religion lest we build our house upon sand."[108] She believes that a postmodern approach is promising for understanding the confusion in debates regarding critical realism. Murphy introduces Imre Lakatos' theory of scientific method as a valuable refinement of postmodern epistemology, as applicable to theology as it to science.[109]

According to Lakatos, scientific endeavours consist of *research programs* which are historically extended and socially embodied.[110] Such programs coalesce around a central theory called the *hard core* and protect this theoretical core through an outer ring of auxiliary hypotheses called the *protective belt.*[111] The function of the protective belt is twofold. First, it provides the subsidiary theories needed to relate the hard core to the experimental data. Second, in the event of a mismatch between the data and the theory, the anomaly can be rectified by modifying the auxiliary hypotheses in the belt rather than the central theory of the core. Thus, the belt protects the core by absorbing the anomalies and giving way *in lieu* of the core. Murphy explains:

> A research program, then, is a temporally extended series of complex theories whose core remains the same while auxiliary hypotheses are successively modified, replaced, or amplified in order to account for problematic observations. The problem in evaluating research programs is that, given enough ingenuity on the part of the scientists, any

---

108 Ibid., 42.

109 Murphy, *Theology in the Age of Scientific Reasoning* (Ithaca, New York: Cornell University Press, 1990).

110 For details, refer to Imre Lakatos, *The Methodology of Scientific Research Programmes* (Cambridge: Cambridge University Press, 1978).

111 Auxiliary hypotheses add enough information to allow empirical data to confirm the theory and form the protective belt. Murphy, *Anglo-American Postmodernity*, 52.

> conflicting datum (anomaly) can be made consistent with the program by adding theoretical explanations.[112]

The strategy of directing anomalies against the belt rather than the core is called the *negative heuristic*. In other words it is "the plan or rule to protect the hard core from falsification by making additions or changes in the belt of auxiliary hypotheses."[113] By contrast, the *positive heuristic* consists of the envisioned experimental and theoretical program which is designed to extend the robustness of the core hypothesis.[114] Since the hard core defines the research program, it is equivalent to the Kuhnian paradigm. Thus, a change in the hard core would imply a change in the research program. So understood, the negative heuristic incorporates the Kuhnian resistance to falsification since anomalies are directed against the protective belt in an attempt to protect the core. With regard to changes in the belt, the research program is considered to be *progressive* if the new auxiliary hypotheses allow for the prediction and discovery of previously unforeseen phenomena in addition to rectifying the anomaly in question.[115] In other words, a research program is said to be progressive when new versions of the program not only account for the anomalies that provoked the changes but are also supported by "novel," hitherto unexpected "facts." On the other hand, when these changes yield nothing beyond the rectification of the offending anomaly, such changes are referred to as *ad hoc*, and the research program is said to be *degenerating*.

112 Nancey Murphy, *Beyond Liberalism and Fundamentalism* (Valley Forge, PA: Trinity Press International, 1996), 101.

113 Murphy, *Theology in the Age of Scientific Reasoning*, 184.

114 Ibid., 185.

115 A research program is said to be progressive when the following three conditions are met: (1) Each new version of the theory (core theory and its auxiliaries) preserves the unrefuted content of its predecessor. (2) Each new version of the theory has excess empirical content over its predecessor; that is, it predicts some novel, hitherto unexpected facts. (3) Some of these predicted facts are corroborated. When the first two conditions are met, then the theory is said to be theoretically progressive; when all three conditions are met, theory is empirically progressive. Murphy, *Anglo-American Postmodernity*, 53.

In other words, a "degenerating research program is one whose core theory is saved by *ad hoc* modifications of the protective belt--mere face-saving devices, or linguistic tricks."[116]

One can see Kuhnian and Popperian influence in the Lakatosian research program. Obviously, according to Lakatos, progressive research programs should be favored over degenerating ones. Consequently, while a research program can always resist direct falsification through *ad hoc* moves, a continual dependence upon such moves will tend to cause a switch to a more progressive research program. This Lakatosian switch is therefore equivalent to both a Kuhnian revolution and a Popperian falsification.[117] Lakatos synthesizes Kuhn with Popper by envisioning falsification on two levels. In regard to the protective belt, falsification proceeds readily in accordance with the logic of Karl Popper. In regard to the hard core, however, falsification is methodologically resisted and therefore, proceeds more slowly in accordance with the logic of Thomas Kuhn.

According to Murphy, Lakatos' methodology can be used in theology. Murphy provides a crucial modification of Lakatos' conception of a "novel fact" so that this method can be used in theology to decide which theological programs are empirically progressive. "A fact is novel if it is one not used in the construction of the theory T that it is taken to confirm. A fact not used in the construction of a theory is one whose existence, relevance to T, or interpretability in light of T is first documented after T is proposed."[118] According to Murphy, Lakatos' methodology adds here a demand for empirical growth. With this methodology, it would be possible to decide between competing theological research programs using criteria which transcend the programs themselves.

Murphy explains the procedure as follows: Lakatos' methodology can be used in theology, since theologians are

116 Murphy, *Beyond Liberalism and Fundamentalism*, 102.

117 Murphy, *Theology in the Age of Scientific Reasoning*, 61-65.

118 Ibid., 68.

tempted to use the same sort of *ad hoc* theorizing as scientists use. In theology, the facts would be evidence from biblical studies, historical data and the sorts of religious experience that are open to communal discernment and agreement. Here, Murphy links her line of thinking with the claims of postmodern theologians like George Lindbeck and Ronald Thiemann, for whom the facts of religious language are the practices of the religious community.[119] Postmodern theologians insist that theological beliefs be governed by the demand for consistency with one another and with these communal practices. In Murphy's understanding, "doctrines play the role of theories. The hard core would be some 'single, synoptic, imaginative judgment' concerning what Christianity is all about."[120] Murphy develops these ideas further into a three-layer epistemological scheme laid out in the book, *On the Moral Nature of the Universe*,[121] combining in an impressive single framework the ideas of Carl Hempel's hypothetico-deductive method, Imre Lakatos' scientific research programs and Alasdair McIntyre's intellectual traditions.[122] Her concern here has been to unify the epistemological method.

Having examined the modern critical realist views of Ian G. Barbour and Arthur Peacocke and the postmodern critical realist view of Nancey Murphy, in the next section, let me address the concern whether critical realism is modern or postmodern.

---

119 Murphy, *Beyond Liberalism and Fundamentalism*, 96-98.

120 David Kelsey, *The Use of Scripture in Recent Theology* (Philadelphia: Fortress Press, 1975), 159.

121 Nancey Murphy and George F.R. Ellis, *On the Moral Nature of the Universe: Theology, Cosmology, and Ethics* (Minneapolis: Fortress Press, 1996).

122 According to Alasdair MacIntyre, a tradition is a historically extended, socially embodied argument about how best to interpret and apply the formative text(s). The overall justification will consist of taking a long-term historical look at how well the conceptual resources of one's tradition have compared with others in resolving intellectual crises. Comparison of these traditions may show that one tradition is clearly superior to another: it may become apparent that one tradition is making progress while its rival has become sterile. For details, refer to Alasdair MacIntyre, "Epistemological Crises, Dramatic Narrative, and the Philosophy of Science," *Monist* 60 (1977): 453-72.

## 2.3 Is Critical Realism Modern or Postmodern?

According to the modern worldview, absolute truth exists. It values rationality and objectivity, consistency and coherence. The French philosopher, Rene Descartes, laid the philosophical foundation of the modern edifice with his focus on doubt, re-appropriating the Augustinian dictum, *Cogito ergo sum* (I think, therefore I am), which conceived human nature as a thinking substance and the human person as an autonomous rational subject.[123] The British philosopher-scientist, Isaac Newton, later provided the scientific framework for modernity based on a mechanistic worldview.[124] The modern mind believes that knowledge is certain, obtainable, rational, and objective.

According to the postmodern worldview, there are no absolutes. This worldview emerged in the 1970s from the rise of deconstruction as a literary theory aimed at dismantling modernity. Deconstruction arose in response to the theory of structuralism which theorized that "cultures develop literary documents--texts--in an attempt to provide structures of meaning by means of which people can make sense out of the meaninglessness of their experience. Literature, therefore, provides categories whereby we can organize and understand our experience of reality."[125] Deconstructionists rejected this view, affirming that meaning is not inherent in the text itself, but emerges as the interpreter enters into dialogue with the text.[126]

123 Stanley J. Grenz, "Star Trek and the Next Generation: Postmodernism and the Future of Evangelical Theology," in *The Challenge of Postmodernism: An Evangelical Engagement*, ed. David S. Dockery (Grand Rapids, MI: Bakers Books, 1995), 90.

124 Job Kozhamthadam, "The Changing Face of Science-Christianity Dialogue: Encouragement, Estrangement, and Engagement," in *Science, Technology and Values*, ed. Job Kozhamthadam (Pune, India: ASSR Publications, 2003), 19.

125 W.L. Reese, "Structuralism," in *Dictionary of Philosophy and Religion*, ed. W.L. Reese (Atlantic Highlands, NJ: Humanities Press International, 1980), 553.

126 Even though, Gadamer is not regarded as a deconstructionist in the postmodern view, for details regarding the hermeneutical theory of interpretation, refer

Millard J. Erickson and David Ray Griffin have delineated four different postmodern schools of thought: deconstructive postmodernism, liberationist postmodernism, constructive postmodernism, and conservative or restorationist post-modernism.[127] Deconstructive postmodernism represents a radical denial of the objectivity assumed in foundationalism. Criteria of internal consistency and coherence are devaluated in this approach. Liberationist postmodernism aims at transforming socio-political structures. Constructive postmodernism attempts to revise and reject the modern worldview by rejecting all metaphysical foundations. Conservative or restorationist postmodernism finds there is much within the premodern and modern worldviews worth retaining. All these postmodern streams attempt to overcome the split between subject and object, and they pursue knowledge without exclusive reliance on an objective foundation.

In general, the Western understanding of modernity is fundamentally grounded in the Cartesian split. While modernity is defined in terms of the split between subject and object, post modernity is explained in terms of overcoming the split. Modernity is regarded as foundationalist whereas, postmodernity non-foundationalist. Moderns establish their foundation on pure reason, sense experience, and a correspondence theory of truth where reality belongs to the object, and subjectivity bows to objectivity. Postmoderns, on the other hand, deny such a foundation in objective reality.[128]

---

to Hans-Georg Gadamer, *Truth and Method*, trans. Garret Barden and John Cumming (New York: Crossroad, 1984).

127 Millard J. Erickson, *Evangelical Interpretation* (Grand Rapids: Baker, 1993), 99-103; David Ray Griffin, *Varieties of Postmodern Theology* (Albany, NY: State University of New York, 1989), 18-23.

128 James W. Sire, an American Christian author, outlines five aspects of postmodernism: (i) Things and events do not have intrinsic meaning. There is only continuous interpretation of the world. (ii) Continuous examination of the world requires a contextual examination; we ourselves are a part of the context. (iii) Interpretation depends not on the text or the author, but on the relative viewpoint and particular values of the interpreter. (iv) Language is not neutral, but relative and value-laden. (v) Language conveys ideology. James

To tighten up the vocabulary somewhat, I plan to employ the terms modernity and postmodernity as descriptions of the cultural ambiance of their respective eras in Western culture. I plan to employ the terms modernism and postmodernism with their respective "... isms" to refer to ideologies, to schools of thought, to prescriptions for thinking. Modernism prescribes modern thought, and postmodernism prescribes postmodern thought. Critical realism grew up and feels most at home in the house of modernity. Some would like to see critical realism make a move into the postmodernist dwelling. Should critical realism change residences? Is this move a good idea?

Nancey Murphy recommends change of residence as she sees the critical realist position as resting upon confusion. On the one hand, critical realism takes a strictly modern foundationalist position. On the other hand, it tries to incorporate a postmodern or postfoundationalist recognition of the sociology of knowledge. The confusion enters when advocates of critical realism claim this position lies at a midpoint between naive realism on the one end, and relativist subjectivism on the other. Murphy rejects the views placing critical realism as a midpoint. She contends that modernity and postmodernity occupy different spaces, and critical realism should sit in only one space rather than straddle two. How does she identify these separate spaces of the modern and the postmodern? What kind of a postmodernism does she advocate?

Murphy draws a sharp distinction between the deconstructive bent of continental forms of postmodernism and the constructive concerns of Anglo-American postmodern thinkers. Of these, deconstructionism requires special attention, as the subjective never bows to the objective. According to the deconstructionist,

---

W. Sire, "Logocentricity and Postmodern Apologetic: On Being a Fool for Christ and an Idiot for Nobody," (paper presented at the Wheaton Theology Conference, April 7-8, 1994), cited in David S. Dockery, "The Challenge of Postmodernism," in *The Challenge of Postmodernism: An Evangelical Engagement*, ed. David S. Dockery (Grand Rapids, MI: Bakers Books, 1995), 14.

knowledge is a construction of human subjectivity. All knowledge includes subjectivity, perspective, pre-understanding, pre-judgment, context, social location, self-interest, creativity, imagination and the will to power. In the deconstructionist approach, language does not refer to objective objects as its referents: words refer only to other words.[129] The deconstructionist treats cognitive claims as texts, texts to be critically interpreted. Critical interpretation begins by breaking the connection between the text and its purported object. Even if the claim of the text refers to an object that is extra-textual, it is the text itself that gets deconstructed.

As a consequence of the text's deconstruction, many interpretations of the text are possible, depending on the readers or readings. Deconstructionists apply this theory to the world as a whole, claiming that there is no one meaning of the world and no transcendent center to reality as a whole. On the basis of these ideas, the French philosopher, Jacques Derrida, argued for the deconstruction of ontological descriptions of reality as well as metaphysical explanations of reality claiming that nothing transcendent inheres in reality but the perspective of the self who interprets reality.[130] Offering a moral twist to Derrida, another French philosopher, Michel Foucault, claimed that every assertion of knowledge is an act of power and a use of power.[131] The American philosopher, Richard Rorty, shifted the classic conception of truth as mind, or language mirroring reality, to interpretation. The postmodernist claimed that knowledge is not rational, objective or mechanistic but historical, relational and personal. According to Peters and Peterson, "Deconstruction dislodges the codes of authority and foundational assumptions

129 Dockery, "The Challenge of Postmodernism," 16.

130 Jacques Derrida, *Of Grammatology*, trans. Gayatri Chakravorty Spivak (Baltimore: Johns Hopkins University Press, 1976), 50.

131 Michel Foucault, "Truth and Power," in *Power/Knowledge: Selected Interviews and Other Writings, 1972-1977*, ed. Colin Gordon (New York: Pantheon, 1980), 133.

such as referential truth claims."[132] In a nutshell, deconstruction is a dynamic ongoing hermeneutic, never resting in a final or static state of interpretation.

Postmodern deconstructionist views have invited criticism from various corners, including scientist theologians. The English theoretical physicist, John Charlton Polkinghorne, is particularly preoccupied by the so-called postmodern dissemination of meaning: "If all meaning is a personal human construct, then God can be no more than a self-selected symbol for our individual highest ideals. Religion might be true for me or true for you, as a technique for living, but it could not be just true, pure, and simple."[133] Many postmodern thinkers distance themselves from the more radical forms and implications of poststructural and deconstructive thought. Murphy advocates a kind of postmodernism which is not deconstructionist. Why?

Critical realism may look like it should be at home within the modern mind furnished with realism, rationality, empirical knowledge, foundationalism, and the correspondence theory of truth. Critical realism is still realism, after all, even if it incorporates perspective and social understanding along with imagination. Murphy would like critical realism to move out of its modern home and into a postmodern one, her Anglo-American postmodernist residence. Because this postmodernist structure is non-foundationalist and relies on a coherence theory of truth. Should critical realism make the move? To encourage this move, Murphy has decorated her postmodernist home with holism. She declares, "Perhaps the clearest and cleanest break with modern thought is the replacement of foundationalism by holism."[134] Holism fits multiple referential claims together into a conceptual web which reinforces each claim. Peters and Peterson write about Murphy's approach: "The correspondence theory of truth is not

132 Peters and Peterson, "The Higgs Boson," 196.

133 John Polkinghorne, *Scientists as Theologians* (London: Society for Promoting Christian Knowledge, 1996), 2-3.

134 Murphy, *Anglo-American Postmodernity,* 26.

replaced but complemented by a coherence version of truth. Coherent truth is not apodictic or absolute or dogmatic; rather, it weighs what seem more coherent assemblages of data over against what seems less coherent."[135] Claims are tested "as a combination of coherence and empirical adequacy...given a stable conceptual system, truth is in part a function of the way the world is."[136] Murphy seems to want both coherence and correspondence, both conceptual construction and empirical reference in her critical realist view.

Murphy recommends a holist postmodernist approach in theology. "Non-foundational theology employs holist justification, which seeks the relation between a disputed belief and the web of interrelated beliefs within which it rests."[137] Murphy says that "postmodern conservative theology must maintain some special role for Scripture over against experience as authority for theology; second, it must provide for special acts of God; and third, it must provide for the possibility of making truth claims for Christianity."[138] Recognizing the circular relationship between theory and facts in science and theology, core beliefs provide the framework for interpreting human experience in general, as well as biblical data. For Murphy:

> The hard core of a research program in systematic or doctrinal theology, therefore, will most likely be one's non-negotiable and most general understanding of God and of God's relation to the created order. The doctrine of the Trinity functions nicely as a core theory for classical orthodoxy, since all of the rest of the Christian doctrines

135 Peters and Peterson, "The Higgs Boson," 197.

136 Nancey Murphy, "The Limits of Pragmatism and the Limits of Realism," *Zygon*, vol. 28 (1993): 354.

137 Murphy, *Anglo-American Postmodernity*, 117.

138 Ibid., 118.

> can be unified by means of their direct or indirect relations to one of the persons of the Trinity.[139]

In Murphy's view, the core doctrine provides the theory that reflects on biblical facts, just as biblical facts are already theory or doctrine-laden. This is a circular interaction, to be sure; but it is still a progressive movement toward expanding or deepening knowledge. Murphy acknowledges, "There is always a degree of circular reasoning involved, but it might be called virtuous rather than vicious circularity."[140]

Is Murphy's holist postmodern epistemology adequate for science-theology dialogue? John Puddefoot criticizes Murphy for relying excessively on empirical verification of theological claims. Murphy "is trying to place the emphasis for theology and science upon yet another version of empiricist foundationalism."[141] Instead Puddefoot affirms, "I would want to emphasize the acts of personal judgment and communal affirmation and reaffirmation that underpin all the knowledge we have of all things, not on the basis of correspondences mysteriously discerned between theories and their referents."[142] Almost in a similar fashion, Grant Gillett calls Murphy to underline the indispensable self-involvement of the person of faith in Christian cognitive claims as more than those made in scientific discourse. According to Gillet, "God is not an object about which we can formulate theories that can be tested for their adequacy against a rather flimsy and remarkably self-authenticating database. God is a person who transcends, creates, and inspires, and who imposes the divine personality on the process of gaining knowledge."[143]

139 Nancey Murphy, Grant Gillett, and John Puddefoot, "What has Theology to Learn from Scientific Methodology," in *Science and Theology: Questions at the Interface,* ed. Murray Rae, Hilary Regan, and John Stenhouse (Grand Rapids MI: William B. Eerdmans Publishing Co., 1994), 106.

140 Murphy, "What has Theology to Learn," 112.

141 Ibid., 145.

142 Ibid.

143 Ibid., 135.

A deeper and objective analysis of Murphy's position reveals that her theological reflection is based on an ultimate faith commitment to God and personal trust in God. Aware of Murphy's view, Peters and Peterson offer a conditional yes to her postmodern critical realist theology. They write:

> Holist postmodernism presents itself as a healthy option, because it seeks to overcome the split between subject and object and retains both in a single epistemology. Deconstructionist postmodernism is less attractive. Even though, deconstructionism aptly points out the distortions in human subjectivity due to social location, its demand that objectivity bow entirely out of the picture of reality seems excessive. Neither science nor theology could adapt to the deconstructionist epistemology.[144]

Philip Clayton sees Murphy's approach (that "modernity is based on three fundamental assumptions or "Cartesian coordinates" and the entire coordinate system is mistaken and should be replaced") as nothing less than leaving modernity behind and developing a "postmodern" approach to theology and science. Clayton critiques Murphy's diagrammatic representations given in *On the Moral Nature of the Universe*, and *Reconciling Theology and Science* where theology stands proudly atop a "hierarchy," the pinnacle of an edifice of knowledge stretching from the physical sciences at the bottom, through the social sciences in one column and the broader natural sciences in another, to theology as the culminating science.[145] According to Clayton, "There is something distinctively unpostmodern about hierarchy drawing and about this hierarchy in particular. It will take a rather large dosage of

144 Peters and Peterson, "The Higgs Boson," 200-201.

145 Murphy and Ellis, *On the Moral Nature of the Universe*, 64-87. Nancey Murphy, *Reconciling Theology and Science: A Radical Reformation Perspective* (Kitchener, Ontario: Pandora Press, 1997), 16f.

metaphysics to make the hierarchy stick."[146] For Murphy, to believe something is to believe that it is true, really true; not just true in a language or true for a speaker. Clayton asks how could one know for certain which statements correspond to the way the world really is? He writes:

> Indeed, demonstrating objectively this or that particular sentence gets things right may exceed our capabilities. Yet this only shows that what the word true means is not identical to the evidence we currently have for thinking that this or that sentence is true. Truth and rationality are not isomorphic. Reasons to believe may always be limited and perspectival, but this fact does not render otiose the claim that true language represents what is ultimately the case.[147]

Personally, I find Murphy's postmodern holist approach more promising in theology as well as in science-theology dialogue. However, the epistemological concerns raised by her approach need to be further clarified. Is Murphy's epistemological holism non-problematic? Does she succeed in avoiding absolutism in her line of thinking? Does she sound as absolutist and dualistic as modernists do, especially in her critique of epistemic foundationalism, the representational-expressivist theory of language and individualism? In spite of providing a postmodern holist epistemology, Murphy is misinterpreted at times as empiricist-foundationalist, and other times as "unpostmodern." Hence, Murphy's postmodern holism needs further attention. A careful construction and explanation of epistemology is of crucial importance for Murphy to provide a rational basis to the use of critical realism while dialoguing between science and theology. For example, social constructivism or postmodern standpoint

146 Philip Clayton, "Shaping the Field of Theology and Science: A Critique of Nancey Murphy," *Zygon,* vol. 34, no. 4 (1999): 612. For details, see p. 598-618.

147 Clayton, "A Critique of Nancey Murphy," 612.

epistemologies, would pluralize knowledge into a multiplicity of incommensurable positions, annihilate the possibility of the unity of knowledge and the concept of grounded truth and thereby undermine the singular universality of the one True God which we intend to defend. I will claim that a fuzzy logical explanation of critical realism (a fuzzy model of critical realism) can provide a mathematical base to improve upon the use of holist postmodern critical realism in science-theology dialogue. The fuzzy model will also provide an inclusive epistemology within a single framework of knowing.

## Conclusion

In this chapter, I have examined the critical realist views of Ian G. Barbour, Arthur Peacocke and Nancey Murphy. Against the modern critical realist views of Barbour and Peacocke, Murphy provides a postmodern critique of critical realism. Critical realism began within the home of the modern mind. Murphy wants critical realism to move out of the modern mind and into the Anglo-American postmodern mind. With Murphy I recommend that critical realism move into the postmodern dwelling; but I further suggest that her holist postmodern epistemology be reconstructed in such a way that the holistic path will not lie at a midpoint between naive realism on the one end, and relativist subjectivism on the other as Murphy fears. Instead, the holistic postmodernist approach, complemented by fuzzy logical model, will provide an act of knowing within a single epistemological framework encompassing diverse horizons of knowledge.

# 3. Fuzzy Model of Critical Realism

Is it possible to have a holistic model for critical realism? In order to address this question, I will use a fuzzy model of critical realism--the model wherein critical realism is complemented by holistic epistemology--based on fuzzy logic. As mentioned in the introductory chapter, fuzzy logic has often been wrongly criticized as "fuzzy" or "vague" due to the use of the word "fuzzy." In reality, fuzzy logic is precise mathematical theory that deals with uncertainty and ambiguity. This logical tool itself is clear and not ambiguous. Mathematically, fuzzy logic helps to deal with different kinds of fuzziness that exist in the real world such as vagueness, impreciseness, inexactness, amorphicity, and randomness. I will demonstrate that a fuzzy model of critical realism will provide a fundamental theoretical framework into which multiple referential claims can be fitted, and thereby provide a mathematical base to improve upon the existing explanations of critical realism. The fuzzy model will also provide a single epistemological framework to enhance science-theology dialogue. Let me first explain the basic concepts of fuzzy logic.

## 3.1 Fuzzy Logic: Fuzzy Sets and Fuzzy Numbers

Although, the history of logic dates back centuries, Aristotelian logic, also known as classical logic, was the most predominant logic that prevailed until the 19th century. The language widely used in classical logic is two-valued logical language. Classical mathematical logic divided the world into "yes and no," "white and black," "true and false."[148] The tradition of classical logic with its bivalent thinking has been with us for a long time. Classical logic demands a correct form of reasoning. In this logic, a true conclusion is made based on true premises only when reasoning is correct. If the premises and forms of reasoning are accurate, then the consequence can be expected to be true. Correct reasoning is paramount in classical logic. In this form of logic, neither the subjective factors of reasoning, nor the imprecise and uncertain account of information are taken into account. It suffers from serious deficiencies in tackling the problems of uncertainty in real life. Humans have held on to this logic for a long time. The emergence of new logics, especially fuzzy logic, has revealed new viewpoints and perspectives to understand complex human realities better.

The emergence of fuzzy thinking can be traced both in western and, much earlier, in non-western philosophies. Zhong Li traces fuzzy concepts in the western philosophies of Heraclitus (things could be simultaneously true and not true) and Plato (third possible region between true and false).[149] However, he locates the more recent re-emergence of the fuzzy concept in the work of the Polish logician Jan Lukasiewicz in the early 1900s. Lukasiewicz worked on the middle "indeterminate" and exhibited a spectrum between falsehood and truth, a continuum between 0 and 1 based on indeterminacy.[150] Li writes:

> It was Lukasiewicz who first proposed a systematic alternative to the bi-valued logic of Aristotle. In the early 1900s, Lukasiewicz described a three-valued logic, along

148 Priyanka Kaushal, Neeraj Mohan and Parvinder S. Sandhu, "Relevancy of Fuzzy Concept in Mathematics," *International Journal of Innovation: Management and Technology*, vol. 1, no. 3 (2010): 312.

149 Zhong Li, *Fuzzy Chaotic Systems: Modeling, Control, and Applications* (Berlin, Germany: Springer-Verlag, 2006), 1.

150 Bart Kosko, *Fuzzy Thinking: The New Science of Fuzzy Logic* (New York: Hyperion, 1993), 19.

> with the mathematics to accompany it. The third value he proposed can best be translated as the term 'possible,' and he assigned it a numeric value between True and False. Eventually, he proposed an entire notion and axiomatic system from which he hoped to derive modern mathematics. Later, he [found], there was no difficulty in deriving an infinite-valued logic. Lukasiewicz felt that three- and infinite-valued logics were the most intriguing, but he ultimately settled on a four-valued logic, because it seemed to be the most easily adaptable to the Aristotelian logic.[151]

Fuzzy logic does not contradict classical logic, nor does it ignore it. Fuzzy logic may be regarded as an advance in classical logic and multi-valued logic which takes into account the details of values. It is an alternative way of reasoning, which considers a spectrum of values often neglected in classical logic. Philosophically fuzzy logic is a logical system and scientifically it is a mathematical system with set theories and membership functions. What is important is that, whether philosophically or scientifically, the nature of fuzzy logic is very different from that of traditional mathematics and logical systems.

The specific term "fuzzy" was used for the first time in the scientific world by Lofti A. Zadeh at the department of electrical engineering at the University of California in Berkeley. In 1965, Zadeh published a paper on "Fuzzy Sets" in which he addressed the problem of natural language in computers.[152] According to Zadeh, the absolute values cannot adequately and accurately represent natural language and other categories in life. Hence, fuzzy logic takes up degrees of truth rather than the absolute cases of true or false (1 or 0) as in classical logic. Fuzzy logic considers 0 and 1 to represent extreme cases of truth as well

151 Li, *Fuzzy Chaotic Systems,* 1.

152 Lofti A. Zadeh, "Fuzzy Sets," *Information and Control,* vol. 8 (1965): 338-363.

as intermediate truth-values to represent the cases in between extremes. As an example, the height of two persons could be assessed as tall, almost tall, very tall, somewhat tall etc.

Fuzzy sets, fuzzy numbers and membership functions, are the main factors of fuzzy logic. Fuzzy sets are characterized by a continuum of grade of membership. Zadeh writes:

> Let **X** be a space of points, with a generic element of **X** denoted by $\boldsymbol{x}$. Thus $\mathbf{X} = \{\boldsymbol{x}\}$. A fuzzy set **A** in **X** is characterized by a membership function $\mu_A(\boldsymbol{x})$ which associates with each point in **X** a real number in the interval **[0, 1]**, with the values of $\mu_A(\boldsymbol{x})$ at $\boldsymbol{x}$ representing the "grade of membership" of $\boldsymbol{x}$ in **A**. Thus, the nearer the value of $\mu_A(\boldsymbol{x})$ to unity, the higher the grade of membership of $\boldsymbol{x}$ in **A.**[153]

Mathematically, the Fuzzy set A in a nonempty set X is characterized by its membership function $\mu_A(x)$: $X \rightarrow [0, 1]$, where $\mu_A$ is described as the membership function of A and $\mu_A(x)$ is interpreted as the degree of membership of the element x in fuzzy set A, for each x belonging to X.[154] The symbol $\rightarrow$ denotes the mapping, whereby each element x of the set X is associated with a value in the unit interval [0, 1]. The value 0 is used to represent complete non-membership and the value 1 is used to represent complete membership and the values in between are used to represent intermediate degrees of membership.

Fuzzy sets are not precise. Membership in a fuzzy set is a matter of degree. The main idea behind a fuzzy set is gradual membership. This better comprehends and represents realities in human life. For example, the set of people who are aged between 35- 40 is crisp, but the set of people who are around forty is fuzzy.

---

153 Zadeh, "Fuzzy Sets," 339.

154 P. Venkata Subba Reddy, "Fuzzy Modelling and Natural Language Processing for Panini's Sanskrit Grammar," *Journal of Computer Science and Engineering*, vol. 1, no. 1 (2010): 99.

As an illustration, consider the following graph (figure 3.1) representing a set of tall people.[155] The horizontal axis refers to the height of persons in feet, and the vertical axis takes the membership values in the unit interval [0, 1].

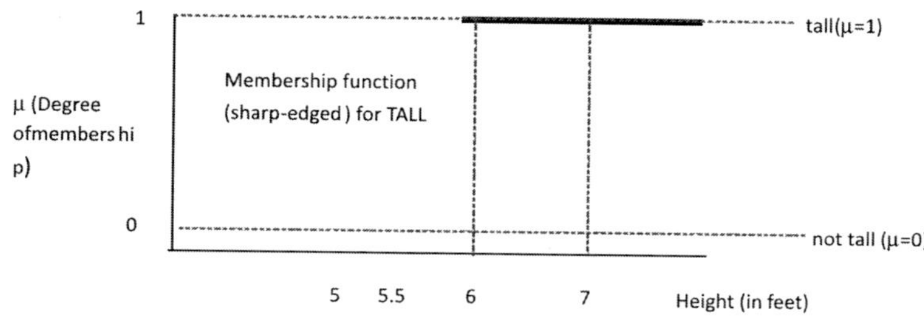


Figure 3.1. Classical set function

We might assess a person as tall if he or she is taller than or equal to 6 feet and not tall if below 6 feet. Such an assessment is based on binary mathematical thinking. In the graph (figure 3.1), the membership values of the height of persons in the fuzzy set of tall people (T) are represented as

$\mu_T(5) = 0, \mu_T(5.5) = 0, \mu_T(6) = 1, \mu_T(7) = 1.$

Only two membership values exist, 0 (not tall) or 1 (tall). No intermediate values are taken into account. For example, there is no distinction between somebody who is 6′5″ (6 feet 5 inches) and someone who is 7′1″ (7 feet 1 inch). Both 6′5″ and 7′1″ are in the same category "tall," even if there exists notable difference between the two heights. As well, consider the difference between someone who is 5′11″ (5 feet 11 inches) and someone who is 6 feet. The former falls in the set of not tall, even if the difference between the two is just one inch. This way of thinking, the binary thinking, does not accurately describe the real world characteristics.

155 Figure as depicted in Reza Piroozfar, "Search of a Justified Decision-Making Process in Urban Planning" (Ph.D. dissertation, Berlin University of Technology, 2012), 107.

In the real world, the set of tall people overlaps. Moreover, the understanding of being tall varies from culture to culture.

Fuzzy logic can represent the set of tall people more accurately. Consider the following graph (figure 3.2) representing the fuzzy set of tall people. The horizontal axis refers to the height of persons in feet, and the vertical axis refers to the membership values in the unit interval [0, 1]. The continuous curve represents the fuzzy set function for Tall.

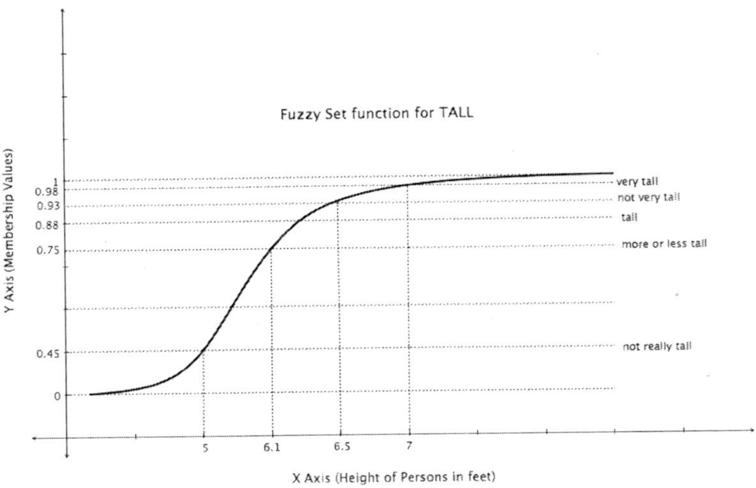


Figure 3.2. Fuzzy set function

Fuzzy logic, unlike classical mathematics, can efficiently represent the membership values of the height of persons within the unit interval [0, 1]. The degree of membership of a person in a fuzzy set of tallness is represented not only by the limiting absolutes, but also by any number from 0 to 1.[156] For example, in the graph (figure 3.2) people who are very tall, not very tall, tall, almost tall, more or less tall, and not really tall will have membership values

156 Singpurwalla, Nozer D. and Jane M. Booker, "Membership Functions and Probability Measures of Fuzzy Sets," *Journal of the American Statistical Association*, vol. 99, no. 467 (2004): 868.

of 0.98, 0.93, 0.75, 0.58, and 0.45, respectively. Mathematically they are represented as

$\mu_T(5) = 0.45$, $\mu_T(5.6) = 0.58$, $\mu_T(6.1) = 0.75$, $\mu_T(6.5) = 0.93$, $\mu_T(7) = 0.98$.

Classical sets consist of objects with precise properties (either true or false, either yes or no, etc.), so their membership values are precise. Fuzzy sets contain imprecise properties (very tall, more or less tall, etc.) consequently their membership values are imprecise.[157] Elements in a fuzzy set can be members of other fuzzy sets on the same horizon as they overlap. The best example is that of a fuzzy number.

A fuzzy number is a set function. The value of a fuzzy number is not as exact or precise as an ordinary single-valued number. Instead, it is a function whose domain is a set where each numerical value in the domain is assigned a "grade of membership."[158] Fuzzy numbers represent the real world better than single-valued numbers. Fuzzy numbers are defined in different ways. The following are representations of different kinds of fuzzy numbers namely, triangular, trapezoidal and normal fuzzy numbers (figures 3.3, 3.4, 3.5).[159] The horizontal axis takes the value in real numbers and the vertical axis takes the membership grade in the interval the unit interval [0, 1]. The shape of the membership function defines the fuzzy set (here the fuzzy number) and the type of the membership function depends on the purpose. The triangular, trapezoid and normal shapes are the most commonly used fuzzy numbers. For example, the triangular fuzzy number can be used to represent time as duration, the trapezoidal to represent the set of healthy people, and normal to represent the average score of students in an exam.

157 Timothy J. Ross and W. Jerry Parkinson, "Fuzzy Set Theory, Fuzzy Logic and Fuzzy Systems," in *Fuzzy Logic and Probability Applications: Bridging the Gap*, ed. Timothy J. Ross, Jane M. Booker, W. Jerry Parkinson (Philadelphia: Society for Industrial and Applied Mathematics, 2002), 30.

158 Robert Fuller, *Fuzzy Reasoning and Fuzzy Optimization* (Turku, Finland: University of Turku and Abo Academy, 1998), 13.

159 Fuller, *Fuzzy Reasoning and Fuzzy Optimization*, 13-14.

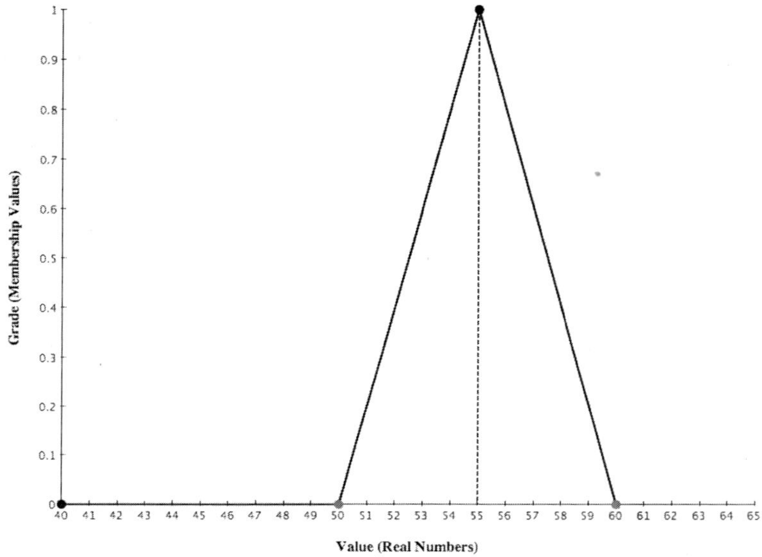


Figure 3.3. Triangular fuzzy number

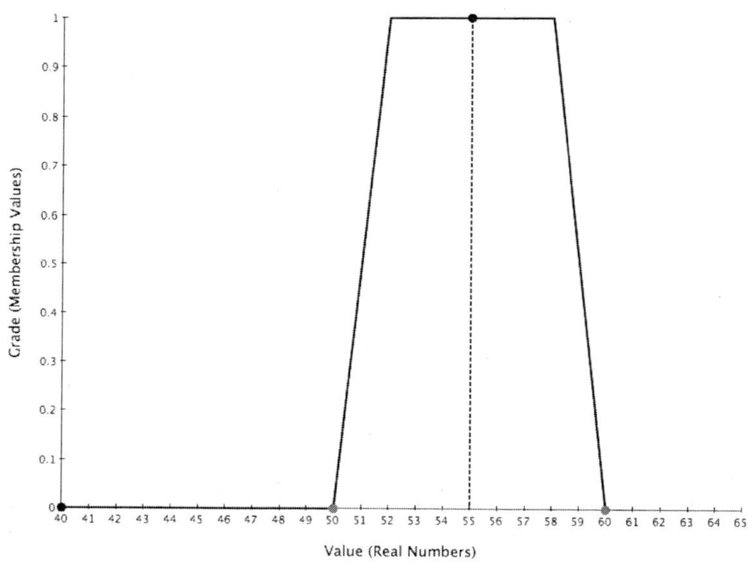


Figure 3.4. Trapezoidal fuzzy number

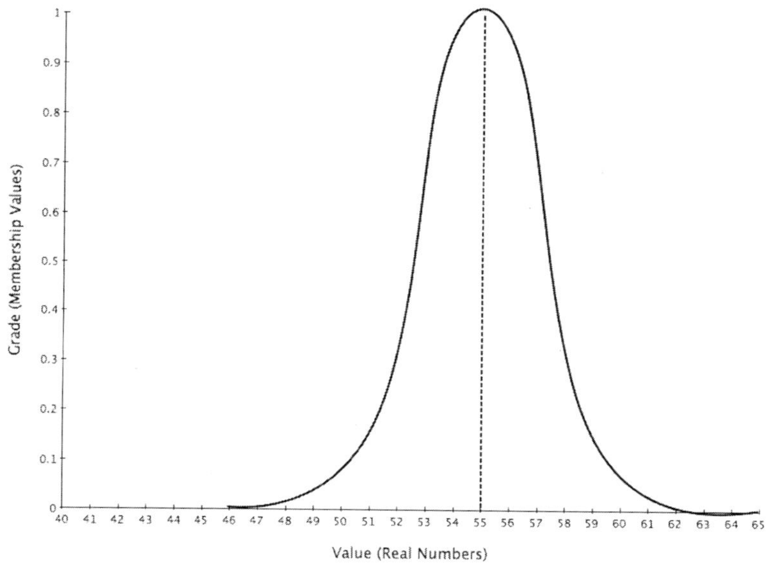


Figure 3.5. Normal fuzzy number

I shall explain the triangular fuzzy number in detail. Consider the following figures of non-fuzzy number 7 (figure 3.6) and the triangular fuzzy number 7 (figure 3.7).[160] In both figures, the horizontal-axis takes the real numbers and the vertical axis takes the membership values in the unit interval [0, 1].

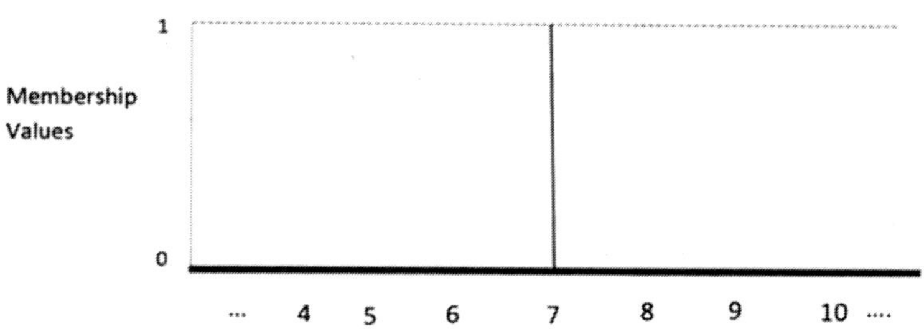


Figure 3.6. Non-fuzzy number 7

160 Kosko,. *Fuzzy Thinking*, 124-125.

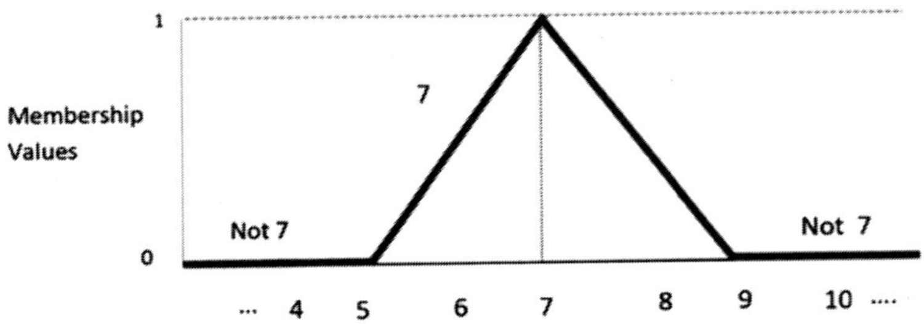


Figure 3.7. Fuzzy number 7

In figure 3.6 above, the non-fuzzy number 7 is single- valued. In this set, 7 belongs 100% to the set 7 and no other number belongs to it. So the membership value of number 7 is 1 and the membership value of every other number is 0. On the other hand, in figure 3.7, the fuzzy-number 7 is a set of multiple-values. The numbers close to 7, or almost 7 or nearly 7 belong to the set 7. They define a spectrum of numbers and some belong more to the set 7 than other numbers.

Having defined and explained fuzzy sets, membership functions and fuzzy numbers, in the next section I shall explain a fuzzy model of critical realism.

## 3.2 Fuzzy Model of Critical Realism

The aim of a fuzzy model of critical realism is to improve upon the prevailing in explanations of critical realism. This model is based on fuzzy logic. In order to explain the fuzzy model of critical realism-- the model wherein critical realism is complemented by holistic epistemology-- I will contrast the ontology and epistemology of fuzzy logic with that of classical logic through the works of Burhan Turksen, who presents the ontological and epistemological differences between classical logic and fuzzy logic. As well, he argues for a hierarchy of levels of theoretical inquiry which includes the ontological, general epistemological, domain-specific epistemological, and application levels.[161]

161 Burhan Turksen, *An Ontological and Epistemological Perspective of Fuzzy Set Theory* (Amsterdam: Elsevier Science, 2006).

The ontological level is foundational. It raises the most foundational questions. What is the nature of truth? Is there an absolute truth? Is truth independent of us? What is our relation to that reality?[162] According to classical logic, absolute truth and a crisply defined reality exists independently of us (Realism),[163] whereas in fuzzy logic, truth is observer-dependent and reality is perception-based, communicated and computed with words whose meaning is represented numerically with continuous memberships. In the classical view, subject is separated from object, but in the fuzzy view, subject and object are not separated but related.[164]

The general epistemological level deals with the nature of human knowing in general and its validity: What is our access to truth or knowledge? How do we acquire knowledge? Absolutely or partially? In the classical view, knowledge is objective, empiricist and certain, while in a fuzzy view, knowledge is subjective and objective, experimental and empiricist.[165] According to the classical view, knowledge, which is objective, is validated by the correspondence theory, in which "a perception or an observation, or a judgment is considered valid or true insofar as it may be shown to match with the objective or factual reality of the world around us."[166] In the fuzzy view, knowledge is validated by approximate reasoning.

The domain-specific epistemological level poses mainly the following questions: What can we know within a specific domain of knowledge? What are the limits or boundaries to it?[167] What are the methodologies used? In the classical modern view,

162 Turksen, *Ontological*, 10-11.

163 Ibid., 17.

164 Subject-object separation is based on Cartesian dualism and the subject-object relation is based on partial membership that means the possibility of a set participating in other sets partially. Ibid., 11, 25.

165 Ibid., 12.

166 Ibid., 20.

167 Ibid., 13.

objective facts and truth are accessible but subjective distortions are neglected (the will, mood and perception of the scientist), whereas, in a fuzzy view, both subjective and objective facts are accessible. The subjective facts are accessible by abstractions and perceptions; their meaning is represented by linguistic variables. In the classical view, a reductionist methodology is used while in the fuzzy view a non-reductionist methodology is used.[168]

At the application level, the classical view emphasizes a linear and mechanistic systems theory of interactions, relations and equations,[169] however the fuzzy view emphasizes humanistic decision and control systems that contain highly non-linear interactions, relations, and equations.[170]

Having contrasted the ontology and epistemology of fuzzy logic with classical logic, I now claim that fuzzy logic is critically realist.[171] Critical realism, by definition, is a view that asserts the mind-dependent and mind-independent aspects of reality. I will claim that fuzzy logic is critically realist in the sense that it is both mind-dependent and mind-independent. Fuzzy logic is mind-independent in the sense that it relies on mathematical rigor, and mind-dependent in the sense that it makes use of imprecise information, intuitive semantic descriptions, inference, abstraction, and approximate reasoning.[172] Its mind-dependent

168 Turksen, *Ontological*, 25.

169 Ibid., 18.

170 Ibid., 25.

171 It is presupposed that critical realism is fuzzy, in the sense that in the critical realist view, reality is both mind-dependent and mind-independent. Objective inquiry, subjective analysis, models, paradigms, metaphors, analogies, etc., make critical realism, whether in science or theology, fuzzy.

172 Fuzzy sets, by definition, are always membership functions which map a universe of objects, say, X onto the interval [0, 1]. Membership of an element in a fuzzy set can be approximate. Fuzzy logic makes use of some intuitively plausible semantic descriptions of imprecise properties to make decisions which resembles human reasoning. An inference model is used while modeling complex abstract systems. Timothy and Parkinson, "Fuzzy Set Theory," 31.

and mind-independent nature makes fuzzy logic critically realist. In sum, fuzzy logic is inherently critical realist.

The best example for showing the critical realist nature of fuzzy logic is the method of defuzzification. "Defuzzification is a mathematical process whereby a fuzzy membership function is reduced to a single scalar quantity that best summarizes the function, if a single scalar value is needed."[173] Witold Pedrycz, Professor at the Department of Electrical and Computer Engineering at the University of Alberta, Canada, writes:

> Defuzzification is an important operation in the theory of fuzzy sets. It transforms fuzzy set information into numeric data information. This operation along with the operation of fuzzification is critical to the design of fuzzy systems as both of these operations provide a nexus between the fuzzy set domain and the real-valued scalar domain. We need the synergy of both these domains to solve many of our ill-posed problems effectively.[174]

There are established techniques to defuzzify the results of a fuzzy system efficiently.[175] The defuzzification method is mostly creative, imaginative and intuitive, based on heuristic ideas such as taking "the action that corresponds to the maximum membership" or "taking the action that is midway between two peaks or at the center of the plateau."[176] The imaginative and intuitive dimensions of fuzzy logic affirm the mind- dependent nature of fuzzy logic.

---

173 Timothy and Parkinson, "Fuzzy Set Theory," 46.

174 Witold Pedrycz, *Granular Computing: An Emerging Paradigm* (Heidelberg, Germany: Physica-Verlag, 2001), 143.

175 Defuzzification is usually carried out using the trapezoid and centroid methods. For details, refer to Timothy and Parkinson, "Fuzzy Set Theory," 45.

176 H. J. Zimmermann, *Fuzzy Set Theory and Its Applications* (Dordrecht, Netherlands: Kluwer Academic, 2001), 232.

The use of fuzzy rules affirms the mind-independent nature of fuzzy logic.[177]

Can fuzzy logic balance modern and postmodern tendencies? Robert John Russell (private communication) is skeptical about my claim that fuzzy logic can provide a balance between Murphy's understanding of modernism and post-modernism. His concern is that, 'according to Murphy, "there can be no midpoint between positions that are not located in the same space." According to Russell, if Murphy is correct my proposal to use fuzzy logic in this way does not work because it requires that all the values it draws on are of a variable that spans a continuous space, like the varying height of people or a swinging pendulum. Of course if Murphy is incorrect, and if modernism and postmodernism are in fact overlapping and partially connected as other scholars such as Peters and Peterson argue, then my proposal might well make sense.' Personally, I go with the latter who regard Murphy's holist postmodernism a healthy option. I will claim that Murphy's holist postmodernism will be more promising if open to Peters and Peterson approach as it can offer an inclusive epistemology even for positions that are not located in the same space as the law of complementarity for fuzzy logic implies overlapping and partial connectivity.

A fuzzy model of critical realism has ties with both modernism and postmodernism. A fuzzy logical model veers toward modernism due to its mathematical rigor and toward postmodernism in its provision for intermediate truth values. Fuzzy logic allows for absolutes (membership values when equal to 0 or 1), but also allows degrees of membership (intermediate truth values). This places the fuzzy logical model in a unique position to combat the extremes of both modernism and postmodernism. This model provides a balance between modernity's over-emphasis on crisp values, and postmodernity's

177 The most used fuzzy rule is the IF-THEN fuzzy rule. For details, see Piroozfar, "Search," 152.

affirmation of relativism, by relying on mathematical rigor while still making room for imprecise information.

Along with absolute values, intermediate truth values and grade of membership functions allow fuzzy logic to add more levels of belonging to the idea of absolutes [0 and 1]. This is in line with holistic postmodernism and in contrast with deconstructive postmodernism, which rejects the possibility of absolutes. Let me explain it further using four-valued logic, which is an example of many-valued logic (or multi-valued logic).[178] Many-valued logic is considered an approach to fuzzy logic.[179] Four-valued logic is considered a discrete case of fuzzy logic. It allows sentences to be true, false, neither or both, as it contains truth value gaps and truth value gluts.[180] Four-valued logic that allows four kinds of truth values will provide a new space of truth values when it is extended to fuzzy logic by incorporating fuzzy set and fuzzy relations in the system of four-valued logic. Fuzzy logic allows a spectrum of truth values such as equally true and equally false, more true than false, more false than true, more than half true,

---

178 Graham Priest, *An Introduction to Non-Classical Logic: From If to Is*, 2nd edition (Cambridge: Cambridge University Press, 2000), 120.

179 Three-valued Logic, four-valued Logic, etc., are examples of many-valued logic. The difference between fuzzy logic and many-valued logic lies in their aims. The multi-valued logical tradition focuses on obtaining valid logical arguments and conclusions using a fixed set of values, logical operators and inference rules, whereas fuzzy logic deals with approximate reasoning, bringing to light a continuum based on indeterminacy, which is a spectrum between falsehood and truth, between 0 and 1. Many-valued logic can be extended to fuzzy logic by incorporating fuzzy sets and fuzzy relations in the system of multi-valued logic. Priyanka, "Relevancy of Fuzzy Concept in Mathematics," 314.

180 Consider the statement "It will rain in Berkeley during the first week of August, 2016." The truth value of this statement is uncertain unless and until the experiment is performed, in this case, till the week is past. Till then the statement remains neither true nor false. Such statements have truth-value gaps. Also consider sentences of the form "This sentence is false." If it is true, then by the meaning of the sentence, it should be false. If the meaning of the sentence is false, then by the claim of the sentence, it remains false. Such sentences have truth value gluts. For details, refer to Priest, An *Introduction to Non-Classical Logic,* 125-130.

more than half false, etc. Hence, fuzzy logical explanation is not reductionist, but holistic as this new space of truth values provides a holistic understanding of reality.

The value of incorporating fuzzy logic into critical realism is that it provides a way to integrate empiricism and subjectivity. In fuzzy logic, a fuzzy set's boundaries are imprecise. A fuzzy set is characterized by a membership function. Fuzzy logicians have made clear that the assignment of membership values and the corresponding truth values of propositions is subjective and local. Jordi Cat, Professor at the department of History and Philosophy of Science, Indiana University, Bloomington, writes about fuzzy empiricism and fuzzy subjectivity to highlight the subjective and empirical dimensions of fuzzy sets and its membership functions:

> It [assignment of membership values] is subjective in all cases because at least one assignment is subjective, namely, to a standard individual, relative to which other individuals get their membership degree. It is subjective because at least that assignment is not based on any inter-subjective, formal or material method of assignment that would ensure consensus. It might, however, not be arbitrary. Instead, especially in the scientific case, it might be guided by background knowledge or assumptions and motivated by certain values. It is based on expert judgment. It is also local, because the assignment of membership degrees varies from context to context.[181]

A fuzzy logical explanation of critical realism that uses a fuzzy model, especially the concepts of fuzzy sets, membership functions, and degrees of truth, improves upon modern and postmodern explanations of critical realism by providing mathematical support. This model provides mathematical strength to the conceptual

181 Jordi Cat, "Philosophical Perspectives on Fuzzy Set-Theoretical Models of Causality," in *Causality: Metaphysics and Methods, Technical Report 19/04*, ed. Julian Reiss (London: London School of Economics, 2004), 4.

web, where multiple referential claims reinforce one another. In this model, the correspondence theory of truth is not replaced but complemented by a coherence theory of truth. Coherent truth is not considered absolute as it takes into account what seems more coherent over what seems less coherent (degrees of truth). This model acknowledges the role of human imagination (intuition, inference) in cognitive claims while reference to objective reality is retained. Every description of reality is constituted by objective referent and subjective interpretive factors within a single holistic understanding of interpretation. Reference to the external or objective world is retained, while subjective constructivism is acknowledged and declared integral to human knowing. Similarly, it supports and substantiates the judgment of Ted Peters and Carl Peterson that critical realism in science is modern in one sense and postmodern/non-foundational in another.[182] The fuzzy model provides a single epistemology (fuzzy epistemology) for critical realism which addresses the binary and relative tendencies adequately. In this holist model, both the subjective and the objective belong together in a single act of knowing, adding many levels of truth to the absolutes.

I have explained how the fuzzy model of critical realism improves upon both modern and postmodern explanations of critical realism. Critical realism can now move into the postmodernist house without disregarding its modern commitment to realism. In the next section, let me explain how the fuzzy model of critical realism enhances science-theology dialogue. First, let me present both science and theology within a single critical realist and fuzzy framework.

182 Peters and Peterson offer the following conclusion: Critical realism in science is modern in the sense that it relies upon rational discourse to describe objective reality, a single universal physical reality. It is postmodern in the sense that it is non-foundational--that is, it recognizes that its view of reality is lodged in creative human mental processes and is, therefore, perspectival, relative, and changing. Peters and Peterson, "The Higgs Boson," 198.

## 3.3 Science-Theology Dialogue within a Fuzzy Paradigm

In this section, I shall first present crisp and fuzzy events within a critical realist framework.[183] In mathematics, we talk about linear and non-linear systems. In a linear system, input causes predict precise output effects. A non-linear system is one in which the output may not be directly linked to initial conditions on account of non-discernible uncertainties. The non-discernable factors (fuzzy factors) which affect the output of the system may be represented by "F" which are independent of the perceived system. In science, we say that the non-linear elements belong to the trans-causal domains and in other higher metaphysical levels they belong to the transcendental domains where the term non-linear is metaphorically equated with fuzzy.

Mathematics provides certain tools for assessing the measure of the "F" elements in a predictive system. The unknowability of the "F" elements implies that they are independent of the perceived system. This independence of non-discernable elements need not exist beyond the realm of human perception. On the other hand, the "F" elements and their independence become meaningful in the context of our perceptions of reality as our judgments are always confined to the context of our perceptions.

The independence of the 'F' factors sets up a renewed context of crispness and fuzziness. In mathematical terms, we define it by a two dimensional (2D) coordinate system (Figure 3.8) where the orthogonal axes represent crisp 'C' and fuzzy 'F'. Any event can be located and identified by a point in this two-dimensional space. The events closer to the crisp axis are determined by discernible elements, which can further be located and classified into the predictive system. For example, matter, rain, doctrine, etc. Those

183 Here, I draw insights from Mori M. Ghomshei, John A. Meech and Reza Naderi, "Fuzzy Logic in a Postmodern Era." Paper presented at Berkeley Initiative in Soft Computing (BISC) special event in honor of Professor Lotfi A. Zadeh at the University of California, Berkeley, Nov. 2-5 (2005). Ghomesheiet *al.* have represented events and horizons within a causality-serendipity framework. In its modified version, I will be presenting events and horizons within a crisp-fuzzy framework adding diverse horizons including science and theology.

events that are in the vicinity of the 'F' axis are not certain, since they are constituted by non-discernible elements which means they cannot be factored into a predictive model. For example, earthquake, love, God, etc. An empirical accumulation of the history of past events can be used as a tool to assess the magnitude of the non-discernible factors as well as to draw the pathways for future events.

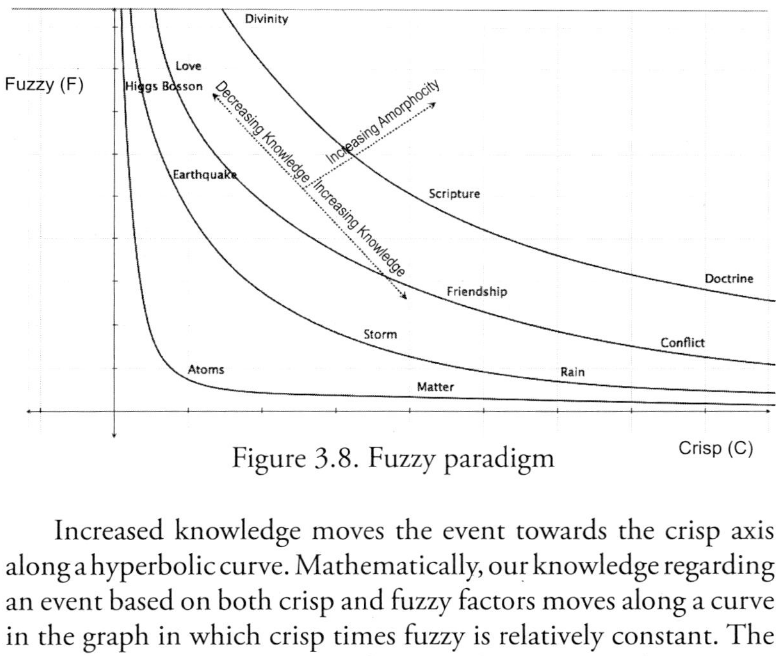


Figure 3.8. Fuzzy paradigm

Increased knowledge moves the event towards the crisp axis along a hyperbolic curve. Mathematically, our knowledge regarding an event based on both crisp and fuzzy factors moves along a curve in the graph in which crisp times fuzzy is relatively constant. The correlation between crisp and fuzzy can be represented as:

$$C.\ F = \lambda$$

The graphical relationship between 'C' and 'F' is inverse; its position depends on the value of $\lambda$. When the value of $\lambda$ goes higher, the curve lies farther from the center of the origin. Various kinds of pathways can be drawn for different types of events. Higher values of $\lambda$ lead to more amorphous events; on the other hand, lower values of $\lambda$ lead to crisp events. An example of a crisp event could be weather patterns where rain is closer to the crisp axis, as its predictability has grown enormously over the past decades. However, earthquakes are rather unpredictable compared to the predictability of rain and other weather patterns, so they are closer to the fuzzy axis.

As shown in the graph, the scale of amorphicity varies for crisp events and fuzzy events. Crisp events, especially natural events, are basically less amorphous, while fuzzy events, those involving human relations and metaphysical beliefs, are more amorphous. In our representation of fuzzy events, amorphicity is not directly linked to crispness. Rather amorphicity is portrayed in a 2-D space, where one dimension takes into account the degree of crispness and the other takes into account the degree of fuzziness. This model provides a mathematical tool for expressing amorphous events by separating crisp events from fuzzy events. Thus, amorphicity is taken as a complexity measure. When complexity increases, amorphicity appears and the event naturally becomes more shapeless. Shapelessness arises from a high degree of complexity. When the interaction of crispness and fuzziness increases, a degree of high complexity (amorphicity) arises.

Events are fuzzy when we do not have sufficient knowledge about the input factors and when the non-discernible elements affect the output. When we are not able to delineate the non-discernable factors of an event, we call the event totally fuzzy. Non-discernible factors of an amorphous event cannot be identified with crispness. When we move from material reality (matter) to metaphysical reality, including human relations, events become more amorphous as shown in the figure. A probabilistic approach may be sufficient for low values of $\lambda$, but a fuzzy logic approach would be highly efficient for dealing with the complexities of an amorphous event. Because probability deals with the occurrence or non-occurrence of the event (randomness), fuzzy logic deals with the meaning of the event. Let me explain.

Figure 3.8 makes clear that diverse horizons are available in the contemporary world and one may generally call them faith horizons as everyone lives by some kind of faith. While a Hindu lives by the Hindu faith, a secular humanist lives by faith in the values and goodness of humanity, a scientific materialist lives by faith in the intelligibility of the world. The scientist's horizon is secular faith, but a religious person's horizon is that of a particular religious tradition. Irrespective of which horizon is adopted, the other non-adopted horizons appear as objects within the chosen horizon. For the one who has adopted the secular horizon of science, different religions appear as objects within that horizon; for a theologian who has made religious faith the encompassing horizon, all other religions as well as disciplines appear as objects within that faith horizon.

The diverse horizons mentioned may be guided by different and conflicting passions and commitments. The conflict would disappear only through conscious attempts at the fusion of horizons and such fusion would be possible only when the concerned horizons are built on complementary, not competing or conflicting, human passions.[184] This is possible between science and theology as the apparent contradictions between the horizons of faith and science are only complementary. The common factor between science and theology is the disinterested search for truth. The reality which each seeks after is the same but attitude of observation and understanding are different for the scientist and the theologian. Science seeks knowledge but the religious quest is for wisdom. Knowledge and wisdom are neither coextensive nor mutually exclusive. But they overlap, in the sense, religion reveals but science explains; science informs, but religion reforms and transforms. Science is a study of causes and religion is an inquiry into meaning. So science and religion are like different sorts of maps, and both help us to get a better picture of reality because each in its own way represents that reality more or less faithfully. Science and theology are two sides of reality and they complement each other.[185]

184 George Karuvelil, "Pragmatism, Existentialism, and Media Theory as Approaches to Religion and Science," *Zygon*, vol. 47, no. 2 (2012): 434.

185 Ted Peters, *Science, Theology and Ethics* (Burlington: Ashgate, 2003), 42.

The challenge is to explore the conflicting passions and commitments by which each horizon is guided, and see whether and how the conflicts are rooted in complementary passions. This attempt takes into account different possible interpretations of data within science and theology, and fuses the horizons by which the meaning of data can be apprehended, which would further give rise to the emergence of new meaning and interpretations. The emergence of new meaning and interpretations are possible in each horizon only when the meaning of the data and events in science and theology interact. The holistic model of fuzzy critical realism helps in drawing the meaning of the data and events in the respective horizons of science and theology which are located in two different locations and enables constructive interaction between them within a single epistemological framework offering new meaning and interpretations. This would provide a better understanding of God, humans and the cosmos.

## Conclusion

In this chapter, I have used a fuzzy model of critical realism, based on fuzzy logic. This model provides a single epistemological framework to enhance science-theology dialogue which holds both coherence and correspondence theories, both conceptual construction and empirical reference. In the next chapter, I shall consider three applications explaining how to fuse the horizons of science and theology to give rise to new meaning and interpretations to fuzzy and amorphous concepts.

# 4. Applications

In this chapter, I would like to apply fuzzy critical realism to two theological concepts and a theological endeavor: Time and eternity, the Trinity and interreligious dialogue. First I will draw a fuzzy logical framework for time and eternity.

## 4.1 A Fuzzy Logical Framework for Time and Eternity

Several scholars have explained the concepts of time and eternity.[186] Applying his extended methodology of 'Creative Mutual Interaction' (CMI), Robert John Russell gives a balanced scientific explanation of time in eternity, and eternity in time.[187] He uses three key concepts for his explanation: duration, co-presence and prolepsis, which he has drawn and interpreted from the German theologian Wolfhart Pannenberg and reconstructed in the light of physics, cosmology and mathematics.

186 For example, Plato regarded eternity as timeless and unchanging. Plotinus understood eternity as the "source of time." Boethius conceived eternity as "the simultaneous and perfect presence of unlimited life." For Augustine, "time is created along with the finite world out of God's timeless eternity." For details, refer to Robert John Russell, *Time in Eternity: Pannenberg, Physics and Eschatology in Creative Mutual Interaction* (Notre Dame, IN: University of Notre Dame Press, 2012), 94-96.

187 CMI incorporates the internal circularities of science and theology within the broader circularity of their mutual interaction as characterized by five upward and three downward paths. The theory is called Creative Mutual Interaction because Russell believes that theology can influence science and *vice versa*. For details, refer to Russell, *Cosmology*, 23.

Duration indicates that time is not point-like. Rather, time involves a temporal thickness, not only in our conscious experience of memory and anticipation, but also in nature, including its fundamental processes.[188] The basis for duration both in consciousness and in the physical world is the temporal structure of eternity. Co-presence, for Russell, is the intrinsic structure of duration in eternity. Here, duration is a differentiated unity which holds together as co-present all events in the history of the universe both now and in the eschatological New Creation.[189] Within the duration of eternity, each event retains its unique past and future. Russell calls this time's "past-present-future structure" or "ppf structure."[190] Within this eternity the distinction between events in time will be sustained while the separation between events in time will be overcome.[191] Prolepsis indicates that "the future is already present and active in the present while remaining future, as exemplified by God's act in raising Jesus from the dead."[192] It is something like a "reaching back" from the eschatological future into our world and history.[193] In the following section, a fuzzy logical framework for Russell's ideas of duration, co-presence and prolepsis is introduced. First, let me consider time in eternity.

188 Russell, *Cosmology*, 313.

189 Russell, *Time in Eternity*, 319.

190 For a detailed explanation of the ppf structure, refer to Russell, *Time in Eternity*, 142-144.

191 Ibid., 319.

192 Russell, *Cosmology*, 313.

193 Eschatological theologian Ted Peters' proleptic thinking is also in the same line. In Peters' view the resurrection of Jesus is the prolepsis of new creation. For him, God is omega and all things will be transformed at the omega coming of the Almighty. He calls this line of thinking retroactive ontology. Ted Peters, *Anticipating Omega: Science, Faith and Our Ultimate Future* (Gottingen: Vandenhoeck & Ruprecht, 2006), 12.

### 4.1.1 A Fuzzy Logical Framework for Time in Eternity

To explain time in eternity using fuzzy logic, let me draw insights from fuzzy sets and fuzzy numbers. As discussed, fuzzy sets have imprecise boundaries.[194] In classical logic, membership of an element in a given set is crisp and well defined. It has only two membership values. To the contrary, an element that is contained in a fuzzy set can have various degrees of membership. Similarly, a fuzzy number is not an exact or single-valued number but a set.[195] As a result, elements in a fuzzy number-as-set can be members of other fuzzy numbers-as-sets in the same horizon..

Metaphorically, the concept of fuzzy number-as-set can be used to explain Russell's idea of co-presence (co-present flowing time). His idea that time is not point-like, but rather involves a duration, is best represented by the concept of a fuzzy number. According to classical physics, time is point-like. Consider the diagram below (figure 4.1). Let $a_1$, $a_2$ represent two events at times $t_{a1}$ and $t_{a2}$ along the horizontal axis. Then $t_{a1}$ and $t_{a2}$ represent two single-valued points which are distinct and separate. Consequently, $a_1$, $a_2$ are imagined as two distinct and separate events in time.

To the contrary, in fuzzy logic, time is not regarded as a single-valued number or point, but as a set whose elements can be a member in another set within the same horizon, as shown in figure 4.2. Let $a$ and $b$ be two events occurring at times $t_a$ and $t_b$ respectively in the horizontal axis. Then $t_a$ and $t_b$ are represented as fuzzy numbers, which are basically fuzzy sets.

194 A fuzzy set is a class of objects with a continuum of grade of membership without sharp boundaries. Membership of an element in a fuzzy set is a matter of degree which can be approximate. For details, refer to Zadeh, "Fuzzy Sets," 338-363.

195 Ibid.

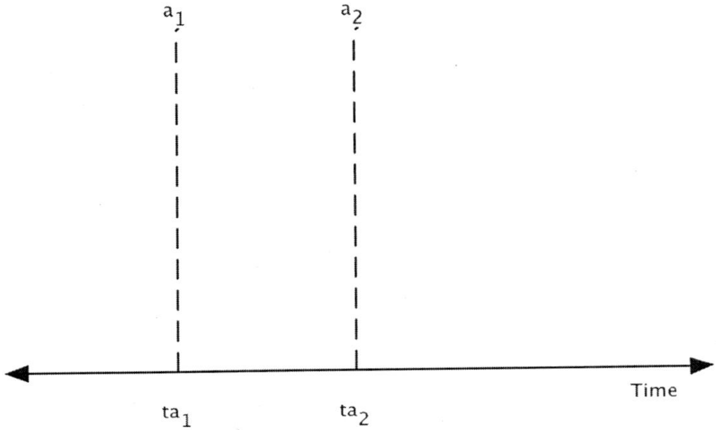


Figure 4.1. Point-like time

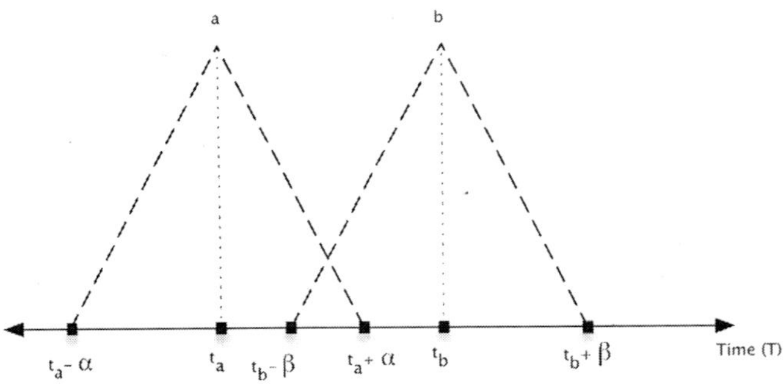


Figure 4.2. Fuzzy time

In the diagram, *a* and *b* are two distinct events, as $t_a$ is distinct from $t_b$. However, in fuzzy logic, unlike classical physics, $t_a$ and $t_b$ have durations respectively, because of their fuzzy membership function. All points between $t_a$- and $t_{a+}$ belong to the fuzzy set of $t_a$ and similarly for $t_b$. The two durations of $t_a$ and $t_b$ share in common all points between $t_b$- and $t_{a+}$. Thus they are distinct but not separate. The same logic can be applied to the events *a* and *b*, leading to the claim that both events partially participate in one another.

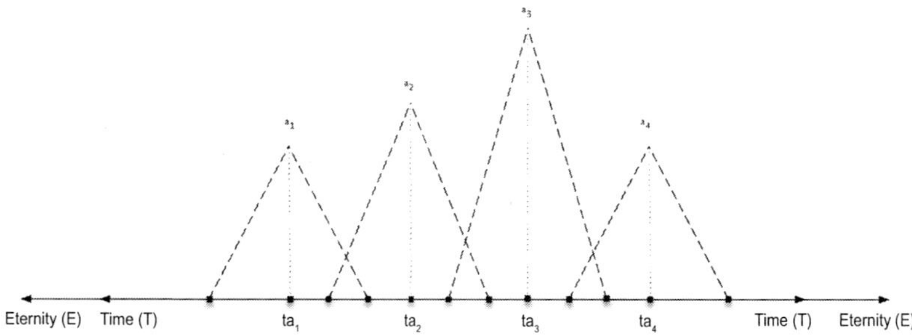


Figure 4.3. Time in eternity

Having examined the fuzzy logical understanding of time, let me now explain the concept of time in eternity. In this explanation I will use Russell's views on time in eternity as co-presence (co-present flowing time) which refers to "a relation between creaturely time (as we know) and the eternity of God [such] that there is a special kind of unity that the ordinary temporal events are given when taken up to the eternity of God."[196] This means that in eternity, all present events, with their distinct past and future, are held together simultaneously. Russell says, "their distinction as unique moments of flowing time is maintained, but their separation into the irretrievable past and unavailable future is overcome."[197] This distinction refers to the past and present of the events as determinate, while the future is indeterminate. As such, time includes a momentary present moment with a distinct and unique past and future. In this understanding of time, the present constantly changes as the possible and indeterminate future becomes a unique present, and then immediately becomes an event in the irretrievable past.[198]As for separation, a particular present separates or divides its past from future. I will explain below how the distinction is maintained and separation overcome in eternity.

196 Russell, *Time in Eternity*, 123.

197 Ibid., 128.

198 Ibid., 124.

Let $a_1$, $a_2$, $a_3$, $a_4$... be different events at corresponding times $t_{a1}, t_{a2}, t_{a3}, t_{a4,...}$ on the horizontal axis of Time (T) which is embedded in Eternity (E) as given below in figure 4.3.

We treat $a_1$ as fuzzy event and $t_{a1}$ as its corresponding fuzzy time. Being fuzzy in nature, $a_1$ participates in the vicinity of $a_2$ and *vice versa* through its temporal thickness or duration. It should be noted that the transitions from $a_1$ to $a_2$ (similarly from $t_{a1}$ to $t_{a2}$), $a_2$ *to* $a_3$ (also from $t_{a2}$ to $t_{a3}$) etc. are gradual, for they are fuzzy sets. The distinction between events is maintained as there is discontinuity between $a_1$ and $a_2$ (also between $t_{a1}$ and $t_{a2}$) due to the difference in the membership values of their elements. Similarly, separation between events is overcome as there is continuity between $a_1$ and $a_2$ (also between $t_{a1}$ and $t_{a2}$) due to the participation of an element of a fuzzy set in the vicinity of another set. From the diagram in figure 4.3, it is obvious that each momentary present has a temporal duration. Each event also has a present moment with its own specific past and future. For example, $a_1$ has a temporal duration $t_{a1}$, $a_2$ has a temporal duration $t_{a2}$, etc.

We conclude that duration is the means of unifying past, present and future by relating them to participate in eternity. The structure of duration is based on the co-presence of all events in eternity. In the divine eternity, all the moments of our life, each with their unique past and present, are simultaneously available. Considered in this way, eternity is neither timelessness nor endless flowing time. Next, I consider eternity in time.

### 4.1.2 A Fuzzy Logical Framework for Eternity in Time

First, I will explain Russell's understanding of the term prolepsis. Prolepsis refers to eternity in time. It signifies "a relation between creaturely time and the eternity of the eschatological new creation as anticipated proleptically in the resurrection of Jesus, which is, in some ways present to Christians now."[199] In prolepsis, the eschatological future determines the present and there is a movement of the ordinary time from creation through its

199 Russell, *Time in Eternity*, 123.

transformation into the eschatological future. Russell views the resurrection of Jesus as an example of prolepsis in ordinary time. I will represent the concept of prolepsis (eternity in time) within a 2-dimensional fuzzy system as given below (figure 4.4) plotting crsip C along the horizontal axis and fuzzy F along the vertical axis, which is based on the diagram given in figure 4.12.

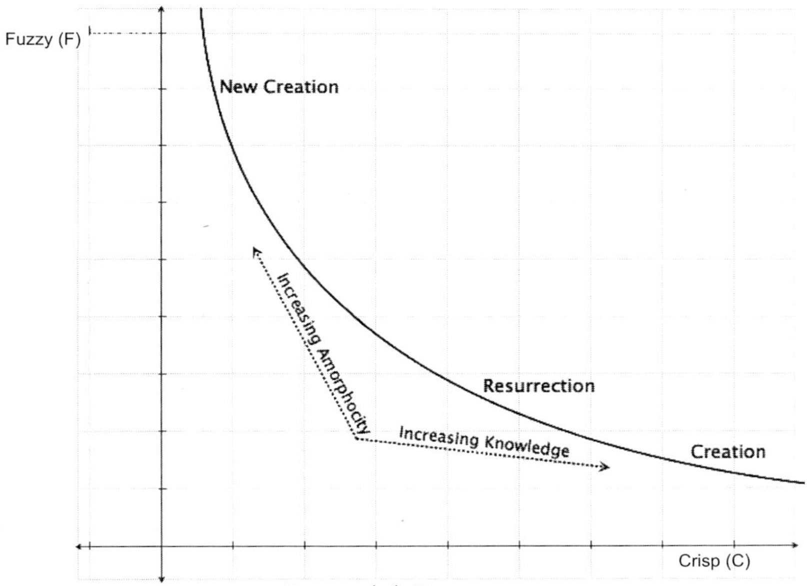


Figure 4.4. Eternity in time

In this diagram, any event can be located and identified by a point on the hyperbolic curve in the 2-dimensional space. Events closer to the horizontal axis can be accessed with epistemological certainty, since they are, to a great extent, predictable. For example, the creaturely things of our lives presuppose a creation. On the one hand, events in the vicinity of the F axis are not discernible, for example, the new creation. Increased knowledge moves an event toward the crisp axis. On the other hand non-predictable and non-discernible factors move an event toward the fuzzy axis, making the event more amorphous. Non-discernible factors (e.g. eternity, resurrection, etc.) of an amorphous event cannot be identified with crispness.[200] Even though, the empirical study of historical events (e.g. Scriptural descriptions, the resurrection of Jesus, etc.) could be considered to a certain extent as comprehending non-discernible elements, their unknowability implies that they are independent of the system. However, this independence of non-discernible factors elements need not exist beyond the realm of human perception. On the other hand, the fuzzy elements. and their independence become meaningful in the context of our perceptions of reality (faith perceptions and their meanings). The placement of the resurrection of Jesus on the hyperbolic curve can be seen in the light of faith.

In Russell's opinion, "God must have created the universe such that it is transformable, that is, that it can be transformed by God's action. In particular, God must have created it with precisely those conditions in order to be transformable by God's new act."[201] He further argues, "Science can be of immense help in understanding the needed conditions and pre-conditions for this transformation. The conditions and characteristics of the present creation which are expected to be continued into the new creation are referred to as "elements of continuity" and those which are not expected to be continued as "elements of discontinuity."[202] As an example, Russell offers hints of continuity and discontinuity from the resurrection of Jesus. The elements of continuity are seen in the fact that the risen Jesus could "be touched, he could eat, break bread, be seen, heard and recognized," whereas the elements of

200 Events become amorphous when crispness meets fuzziness. Amorphicity is a measure of complexity.

201 Russell, *Time in Eternity*, 180.

202 Russell proposes an invert relationship of continuity within discontinuity. "The elements of continuity will be present, but within a more radical and underlying discontinuity as is denoted by the transformation of the universe by a new act of God *ex vetera*. With this inversion, discontinuity as fundamental signals the break with naturalistic and reductionistic views such as 'physical eschatology,' while continuity, even if secondary, eliminates "two-world" eschatology." Russell, *Cosmology*, 309.

discontinuity are manifested in the encounters with the risen Lord beyond the normal limitations of physicality. According to Russell, "these instances of 'realized eschatology' are suggestive of an extended 'domain' of the New Creation proleptically within the old, a domain which ceases with the ascension, but which, when present, includes Jesus, the disciples, and their surroundings."[203] The resurrection of Jesus is believed to be the manifestation of the eschaton in this creation and may be analogically associated with the transformation of the universe.

When the eschatological future appears in the present, ordinary time will be taken into eternity. The transformation of this creation into the New Creation is not an abrupt transition but a gradual and continuous, as the hyperbolic curve. The example of fuzzy sets helps us to comprehend the process of transformation as a gradual process, just as the transition of an element that contains a fuzzy set is gradual, as explained above. In a fuzzy view, events remain distinct but not separate. The elements of continuity (e.g. love and community in this creation) will be present in the transformed universe but within a more radical discontinuity (e.g. without sin or violence).[204]

Back to the graph in figure 4.4, the New Creation is placed near to and high along the vertical axis, because of its uncertain epistemological nature. This provides a whole function, represented

---

203 Ibid., 312.

204 Russell, *Time in Eternity,* 182-183. Other scholars explain continuity and discontinuity variously. John Polkinghorne introduces his meta-scientific insight to explain the transmutation of matter (continuities between the old creation and the new creation). He brings to light two complementary modes of reality to explain the complex process of continuity. One deals with energy and the other deals with pattern, which means the formation of interrelated structures by which a top-down causality of the whole acts upon the parts. John Polkinghorne, "Eschatology: Some Questions and Some Insights from Science," in *The End of the World and the Ends of God*, ed. John Polkinghorne and Michael Welker (Harrisburg, PA: Trinity Press International, 2000), 37. David Wilkinson introduces transformation of matter, adding context to 'matter-energy-pattern-information.' David Wilkinson, *Christian Eschatology and the Physical Universe* (London: T & T Clark International, 2010), 137.

as C. F=λ, determining the events in creation to move toward the New Creation through resurrection. The symbolic function C. F=λ (C is the variable of crisp elements, F the variable for fuzzy elements, and is whatever determinate value) governs the trend of past-present-future of events in time leading them to the New Creation.[205] In other terms, eschatology participates in temporal events by affecting the unifying function governing both creaturely and eternal events in continuity and discontinuity.

## 4.2 Fuzzy Logical Explanation of the Trinity

Although, the word "Trinity" does not appear in the Bible, one can infer the idea of Trinity from both the Hebrew and Christian Scriptures.[206] The Christian inheritance of the Jewish faith posed difficult questions for them after they encountered the divine in Jesus.[207] Eventually, they had to face the dangers of tritheism and modalism regarding the personal distinctions and identity within the Trinity.[208] In this context, the apostolic Fathers, Christian writers of the 1st and 2nd centuries, formulated the Trinitarian doctrine. Since then, several theologians, attempted in diverse ways

205 The function C. F= λ is explained in figure 4.8.

206 God is presented as "Father," "Wisdom," or "Word" and "Spirit" in the Hebrew Scriptures, which indicates a Trinitarian direction. Gerald O'Collins, *The Tripersonal God: Understanding and Interpreting the Trinity* (New York: Paulist Press, 1999), 12-13. The diverse references to God, Jesus, and the Spirit found in the Christian Scriptures were later systematized into the idea of a Trinity. Abbe Felix Klein, *The Doctrine of the Trinity*, trans. Daniel J. Sullivan (New York: P.J. Kennedy and Sons, 1940), 54. For details, refer to p. 54-69. Tertullian is the first Christian writer to apply the word Trinity (*Trinitas*) to God, and the first to develop the formula of one substance (*substantia; ousia*) in three persons (*hypostases*). Yves Congar, *I Believe in the Holy Spirit*, Vol. III, trans. David Smith (New York: The Seabury Press, 1980), 20.

207 Collins, *The Tripersonal God*, 86.

208 Tritheism sacrificed the vital identity of the Father, the Son and the Holy Spirit to their multiplicity. Michael O'Carrol, *Trinitas: A Theological Encyclopedia of the Holy Trinity* (Collegeville, MN: The Liturgical Press, 1987), 212. Modalism is a form of monarchianism that denies separate persons in God in order to safeguard monotheism. Carrol, *Trinitas,* 162.

to reconcile the Trinitarian paradox of "unity with distinction." How to reconcile the unity and distinction between persons in the Trinity? Despite the objections of scholars like Ted Peters, many in the Christian tradition have thought of the mystery of the Trinity as a problem of arithmetic:[209] how can one be three and how can three be one? How do we resolve this paradox? I will show, with reference to the explanations of the Trinity by Basil of Caesarea (330 CE - 379 CE) and Gregory of Nyssa (335 CE – 394 CE), that most of the approaches to understanding the Trinitarian paradox have been philosophical, and still the Trinity remains paradoxical. In this section, I claim that, better than philosophy and binary thinking, fuzzy logic/ fuzzy thinking can provide a critical realist approach to effectively address the Trinitarian paradox.

### 4.2.1 Basil of Caesarea's Explanation of the Trinity

Basil, one of the main architects of pro-Nicene theology,[210] addresses the problematic concerns about *homoousios* which preoccupied most theologians in the fourth century.[211] For example, Basil of Ancyra in the Ancyran synodical letter of 358, expresses his concerns that *homoousios* implies Father and

209 According to Ted Peters, often the Christian educators appeal the Trinitarian paradox to divine ineffability, claiming that this mysterious mathematical trick belongs to the realm of divine incomprehensibility. Peters says; "I have two problems with this approach. For, this trivializes the concept of ineffability. In order to cover our own fuzzy thinking, we ascribe it to the divine mystery. God should not be blamed for confused theology. Second, this approach to Trinity devolves into a problem of arithmetic." Ted Peters, *God the World's Future: Systematic Theology for New Era*, 2nd edition (Minneapolis: Fortress Press, 2000), 19.

210 The first council of Nicaea was held in 325 CE. The Original Nicene Creed (Profession of Faith) was adopted in this Council.

211 Origen, born at Alexandria about 185 CE, was one of the greatest and most influential theologians of the East. Origen emphasizes the one substance and three persons. Origen is the first to use the word *homoousios* in speaking of the Son's basic relationship with the Father. Edmund J. Fortman, *The Triune God* (Philadelphia: Westminster Press, 1972), 56.

Son are of identical ontological status.[212] For him, *homoousios* is unacceptable because it implies the existence of two ultimate principles. For Basil of Caesarea, to speak of Father and Son as having the same *ousia* would be to ignore the differences that follow from the Son being the sort of *ousia* he is, being generated from the Father, and to present him as logically another God.[213] Basil focuses on articulating a mature distinction between a unitary shared nature at one level, and the personal distinctions of Father, Son and Spirit at another. He seems to view the relationship between Father and Son in a fundamentally *homoousian* way: "The Father generates the being of the Son in such a way that there is a mysterious unity between them, and yet the Son's existence as generated qualifies his existence as in some manner distinct from the Father's."[214] Focusing on the community of essence, Basil writes: "According to this, divinity (θεότης) is one. That is to say, it is according to the rationale (λόγος) of the substance (*ousia*) that the unity is thought, but, as in number (αριθμός), the difference of each rests in the particular properties and in the particular characteristics."[215]

Basil speaks of unity of essence at one level and differentiation at another level. Eunomius of Cyzicus (393 CE), one of the advocates of Arianism, insisted that likeness according to essence is logically incoherent - and that, hence, there is only sameness or difference in essence.[216] Against this Basil articulates "a distinction between natures and individuated realities that enables him to assert the Father and Son are, indeed, the same in essence, but distinct at another level thus preserving a certain order among

212 Lewis Ayres, *Nicea and Its Legacy: An Approach to Fourth Century Trinitarian Theology* (Oxford: Oxford University Press, 2004), 190.

213 Basil of Caesarea, *Letters,* no. 361, cited in Ayres, *Nicea and Its Legacy,* 190.

214 Basil, *Letters,* no. 361, cited in Ayres, *Nicea and Its Legacy,* 191.

215 Basil, *Contra Eunomium,* 1. 19, quoted in Ayres, *Nicea and Its Legacy,* 194.

216 Eunomius of Cyzicus, *Apology,* 10. 21-22, cited in Ayres, *Nicea and Its Legacy,* 195.

other persons."[217] Basil distinguishes the unknowability of the divine essence and the knowability of the particular characteristics of Father and Son. To explain it further he uses the term *epinoia*, the "activity of reflecting on and identifying the distinct qualities or properties of something."[218] Basil argues that "unlike the divine essence and power, the energies are diverse, possibly temporary and provide the context within which *epinoia* can distinguish essence and particulars."[219] He provides an extensive account of the distinction between substance and particularities. Even if particularities are added on to the substance, the identity in nature of the substance is maintained. As an example, Basil says, deity is common, fatherhood and sonship are individualities.[220]

In letter 52 (c. 370), Basil writes:

> Since, therefore, the Father is light without beginning, and the Son is begotten light, yet one is light and the other is light, they (the Fathers of Nicea) rightly declared them *homoousios*... For things which are brothers to one another cannot be *homoousios*, as some have supposed; on the contrary, when both the cause and that which has its existence from the cause are of the same existence, they are said to be *homoousios*.[221]

Basil's concern for the identity and difference between Father and Son is both epistemological and ontological. Basil's point implies a metaphysics (at least analogically), but the metaphysical distinction he makes is only vaguely defined in comparison with the precise epistemology which drives the clarity of the distinction. Basil provides unity at one level (of substance) and distinction at another level (of particularities and characteristics). Can we

217 Basil, *Contra Eunomium*, 1. 20, cited in Ayres, *Nicea and Its Legacy*, 195.

218 Ayres, *Nicea and Its Legacy*, 191.

219 Basil of Caesarea, *On the Holy Spirit*, 7.19, cited in Ayres, *Nicea and Its Legacy*, 196.

220 Basil, *Contra Eunomium*, 2.28, cited in Ayres, *Nicea and Its Legacy*, 199.

221 Basil, *Letters*, no. 52, cited in Ayres, *Nicea and Its Legacy*, 205.

explain "unity and distinction" at the same level while sustaining a certain order among persons in the Trinity? I turn to Gregory of Nyssa's explanation of the Trinity to address this question.

### 4.2.2 Gregory of Nyssa's Explanation of the Trinity

Gregory of Nyssa uses an account of God's unitary power, activity, and causality as the basis for comprehending the paradox of divine diversity and unity. Through his employment of a terminology of power, Gregory offers an ontological and epistemological foundation for human knowledge of God that sets the stage for any analogical description of the Godhead. According to Gregory, we do not speak of three Gods because natures are not divisible. The names for the divine nature do not describe God directly, but each one describes the action of God: the divine nature remains unknown.[222] One divine power is constituted by Father, Son and Spirit fulfilling their roles in every unitary divine action. For Gregory, "all divine attributes should be spoken of in the singular and that the persons may be differentiated by us only according to their causal relationships."[223] Gregory's theology can be summarized as follows. Natures are not divisible. Natures and their intrinsic powers are known by the operations of those powers, and the divine operation is always observed to be one. Therefore, divine power and nature are indivisibly one.

Gregory makes a cosmological conception of the indivisibility of natures. He writes:

> The creation is the act of God's power and follows an ordered sequence in which God, after creating dark unformed matter, endows the dark matter with the light and fire of his own power. Then, through the delegated action of this power, individual natures come into being. The Word infuses a power into the creation which, in line with God's will, and mirroring the divine power,

222 Ayres, *Nicea and Its Legacy*, 347.

223 Ibid., 348.

> diversifies into a variety of distinct and unitary natures each with its own 'natural, divinely endowed power.'[224]

For Gregory, the unitary and the simple divine power is intrinsic to the indivisible divine nature. Gregory's argument is that Godhead is itself a term which "originates in observation of the divine activity of seeing or contemplating. However, Father, Son, and Spirit all seem to be engaged in the same activity of seeing and contemplating."[225] For Gregory, "if the activities of the three are the same, then the power which gave rise to them is the same and the ineffable divine nature in which that power is inherent must also be one."[226]

Gregory explains the distinction between the inseparable union of the divine persons in their activity with an account of divine causality. He talks of the power or action of God "issuing from the Father as from a spring, (being) brought into operation by the Son, and perfecting its grace by the power of the Spirit."[227] Gregory uses his model of causality to present the three not as possessing distinct actions, but as together constituting just one distinct action (because they are one power). He insists that the order we perceive in Scriptural discussions of the Trinity does not involve spatial or temporal separation or sequences because of the unity and simplicity of the divine essence.[228] Similarly, each person possesses the fullness of the Godhead; there are no degrees in being God. This means that one cannot assume an ontological subordinationism in Gregory's understanding of Trinity.

---

224 John F. Callahan, "Greek Philosophy and the Cappadocian Cosmology," *Dumbarton Oaks Papers*, vol. 12 (1958), 29-58, cited in Ayres, *Nicea and Its Legacy*, 350-51.

225 Gregory of Nyssa, *On Not Three Gods to Alabius*, 44, cited in Ayres, *Nicea and Its Legacy*, 355.

226 Ibid.

227 Gregory, *On Not Three Gods to Alabius*, 50, cited in Ayres, *Nicea and Its Legacy*, 357.

228 Ayres, *Nicea and Its Legacy*, 362.

Like Basil, Gregory's explanations operate at two levels. Gregory provides ontological unity at one level (of nature, power and action), and distinction between persons at another level (of causality). Even when Gregory speaks about causal differences between the persons in Trinity, he claims that there are no degrees in being God, but Basil, while arguing for substantial unity, preserves a certain order among persons in Trinity. How can we understand this paradox of "unity and distinction," while maintaining "no degrees in being God" and "certain order among persons" in Trinity? I will claim that fuzzy thinking can efficiently address this paradox mathematically.

### 4.2.3 Fuzzy Logical Explanation of the Trinity

I would like to make use of the fuzzy subsethood theorem and the idea of fuzzy containment to explain the Trinitarian paradox of unity with distinction.[229] First, let me explain the subsethood theorem for classical mathematics whose underlying basis is the "whole-part relation." Every whole contains the part, but do the parts contain the whole? In general, the part differs from the whole. According to classical mathematics, a set A is said to be a proper subset of a large set X if and only if A is contained in X. In this case, the part A cannot totally contain X, unless the part equals the whole, but it always partially contains the whole. The idea of "whole in the part" is defined in classical mathematics by drawing insights from statistical probability. The probability of the part refers to the degree to which the subset A contains the whole set X.[230] In other words, the probability of a set or event

229 Fuzzy containment refers to how much one thing contains another thing, or how much one set contains another set. Fuzzy subsethood refers to the degree to which one set is a subset of another. Kosko, *Fuzzy Thinking,* 55.

230 The subsethood relation in classical mathematics is defined as follows: Let S (X, A) stand for the degree to which X is a subset of A. Since A is a total subset of X, S (A, X) = 1. But in general, the converse subsethood S (X, A) falls between the bivalent extremes: $0 < S(X, A) < 1$. Suppose X contains N trials and A contains $N_A$ successful trials. Then the subsethood theorem implies that

A equals the degree to which the part A contains the whole set X, that is, the probability how much the whole X sticks in or fits in part A. If we associate the degree of probability to a value in the unit interval [0, 1], then the probability of the subset A containing the whole set X will be a value between 0 and 1, unless the part equals the whole. According to classical mathematics, the part partially contains the whole. The part cannot totally contain the whole.

The subsethood theorem for fuzzy logic is entirely different from and opposed to classical mathematics. According to the fuzzy subsethood theorem, the whole set can also be contained in any of its subsets. Bart Kosko, Professor of Engineering at the University of Southern California, proved the fuzzy subsethood theorem drawing insights from fuzzy set operations (the different ways sets are combined to form other sets). He observed that fuzzy set operations function differently from classical set operations. Consider the following set operations, namely union ($\cup$), intersection ($\cap$) and complement of a set ($^c$) in classical logic and fuzzy logic. Let A and B be two sets in classical logic. Then the *union* of two sets A and B is the collection of points which are in A or in B, or in both A and B. For example,

Let A = {1, 2, 3, 4, 5, 6} and B= {5, 6, 7, 8}, then mathematically,

A union B (denoted as $A \cup B$) = {1, 2, 3, 4, 5, 6, 7, 8}.

The intersection of A and B is the collection of those elements which appear both in A and B. In the above example, mathematically,

A intersection B (denoted as $A \cap B$) = {5, 6}.

---

$$S(X, A) = \frac{\text{number of elements in } A \cap X}{\text{number of elements in } X} = \frac{N_A}{N}$$

$$= \frac{N_A}{N}$$

where, X contains N trials and A contains $N_A$ successful trials. Here refers to elements which are common to both A and X. In statistics, the above representation of S is known as conditional probability. Kosko, *Fuzzy Thinking,* 60.

A complement of set A is the set of elements not in the set A, but in the whole set X. For example,

Let A = {3, 4, 5} and X = {1, 2, 3, 4, 5, 6, 7, 8},

Then the complement of A (denoted as $A^c$)= {1, 2, 6, 7, 8}.

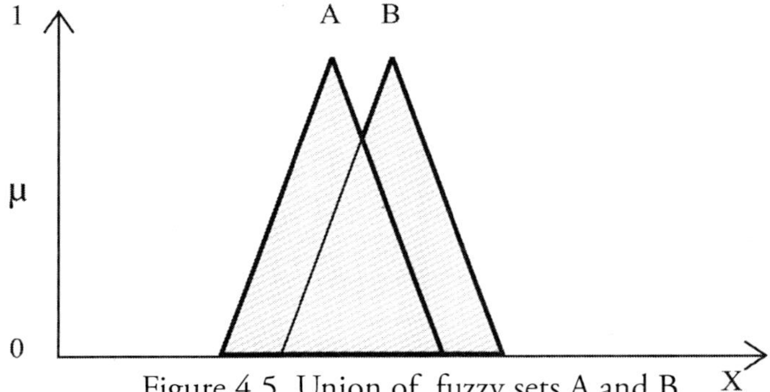


Figure 4.5. Union of fuzzy sets A and B

Now, consider these set operations in fuzzy logic. With due regard given to the membership functions, the fuzzy set operations of union and intersection look similar to those of classical mathematics, while the complementary operations of fuzzy logic are different. Given (figures 4.5 and 4.6) are the diagrammatic representations (*Venn* Diagrams) of the operations union, intersection and complement for fuzzy sets where A and B are two fuzzy sets along the horizontal X-axis and their corresponding membership values are along the vertical axis in the unit interval [0, 1].[231]

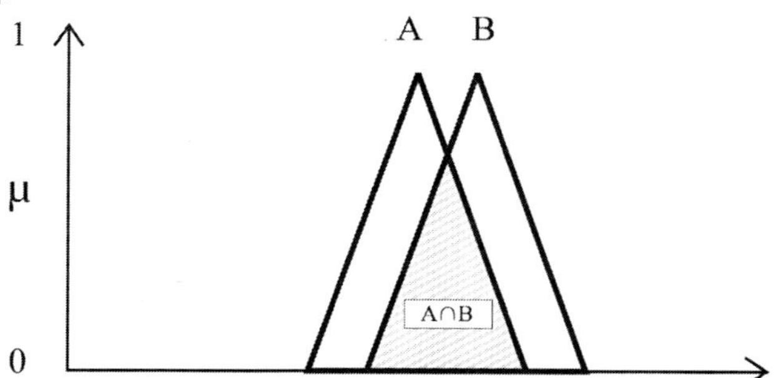


Figure 4.6. Intersection of fuzzy sets A and B

231 Kosko, *Fuzzy Thinking,* 33.

All operations on classical sets hold true for fuzzy sets, except for the complement. In classical mathematics, the union of A and its complement is the whole set, and the intersection of A and its complement is the empty set, denoted as follows:

$$A \cup A^c = X,$$
$$A \cap A^c = \emptyset$$

To explain further, consider the above example where A = {3, 4, 5} and X = {1, 2, 3, 4, 5, 6, 7, 8},

Then the complement of A (denoted as $A^c$) = {1, 2, 6, 7, 8}.

It implies, $A \cup A^c = \{1, 2, 3, 4, 5, 6, 7, 8\} = X$,

Similarly, $A \cap A^c$ = empty set = ø

However, the complementary law does not hold for fuzzy sets because fuzzy sets can overlap, a set and its complement can also overlap.[232] This implies that the union of a set and its complement is not equal to the whole set. Similarly, the intersection of a set and its complement is not an empty set. Mathematically it is denoted as

$$A \cup A^c \neq X,$$
$$A \cap A^c \neq \emptyset$$

Consider the following example (figure 4 .7) of a fuzzy set A. The belongingness of each element *a*, *b*, *c* on the horizontal axis to the fuzzy set A can be represented using membership values in the unit interval [0, 1] along the vertical axis.

Suppose, $\mu_A$ is described as the membership function of A, and $\mu_A(a)$ is interpreted as the degree of membership of the element *a* in fuzzy set A, then in the above graph we have $\mu_A(a) = 1$. This means *a* belongs 100% to the fuzzy set A, and it belongs 0% to the complement of the fuzzy set A, denoted as $A^c$. Similarly, the degree of membership of the element *b* in fuzzy set A is denoted as $\mu_A(b) = 0.4$, which means that *b* belongs 40% to the fuzzy set A, and *b* belongs 60% to $A^c$. The degree of membership of the

232 Timothy and Parkinson, "Fuzzy Set Theory," 34.

element *c* in fuzzy set A is denoted as $\mu_A(c) = 0$, which means that*c* does not belong to A at all, but *c* belongs 100% to $A^c$. This approach illustrates the novelty of fuzzy logic.

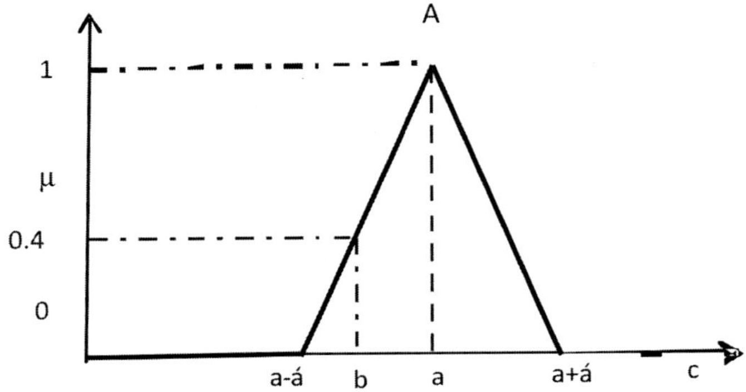


Figure 4.7. Fuzzy set A and its membership values

Mathematically, the complementary value of an element can be obtained by subtracting its membership value from the total membership value 1. Thus we have,

Complementary value of a = 1- $\mu_A$(a) =' 1- 1 = 0.

Complimentary value of b = 1- $\mu_A$(b) = 1- 0.4 = 0.6

Complimentary value of c = 1- $\mu_A$(c) = 1- 0 = 1, where the "-" sign stands for subtraction.

According to fuzzy set operations, the union of a set and its complementary is the maximum of the membership value. The intersection of a set and its complement is the minimum of their membership values.[233] Consider the union of the element *b* and its complementary set, then

$\mu_A(b) \cup (\mu_A(b))^c$ = Maximum of $(\mu_A(b), (\mu_A(b))^c)$ = Max (0.4, 0.6) = 0.6

$\mu_A(b) \cap (\mu_A(b))^c$ = Minimum of $(\mu_A(b), (\mu_A(b))^c)$ = Min (0.4, 0.6) = 0.4

233 Timothy and Parkinson, "Fuzzy Set Theory," 35.

Further, this implies that the union of a set and its complement is not equal to the whole set. Similarly, the intersection of a set and its complement is not the empty set. Because fuzzy sets can overlap, a set and its complement can also overlap. This is the novelty of fuzzy sets. Kosko represented it diagrammatically as given below, where the horizontal axis takes the elements x of the fuzzy set A, and the vertical axis takes up their corresponding membership values in the unit interval [0, 1].[234]

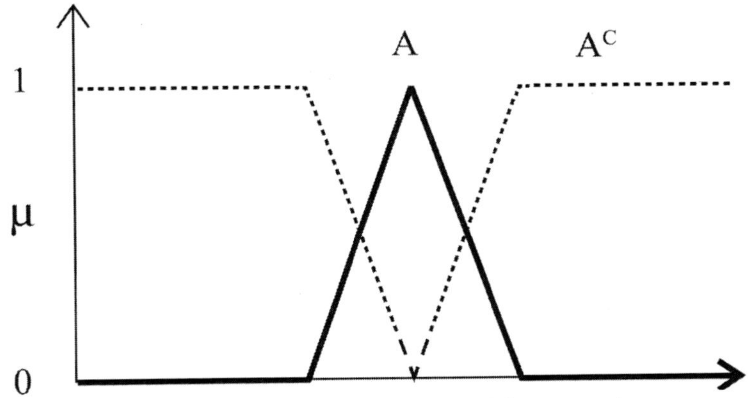


Figure 4.8. Complement of fuzzy set A

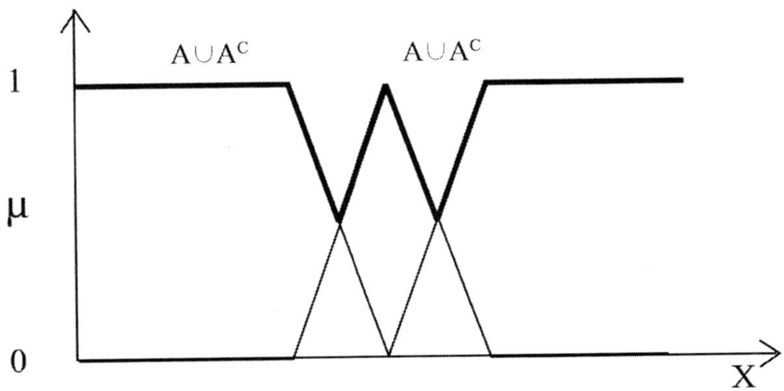


Figure 4.9. Fuzzy set $A \cup A^c \neq$ The whole set

234 Ibid., 34.

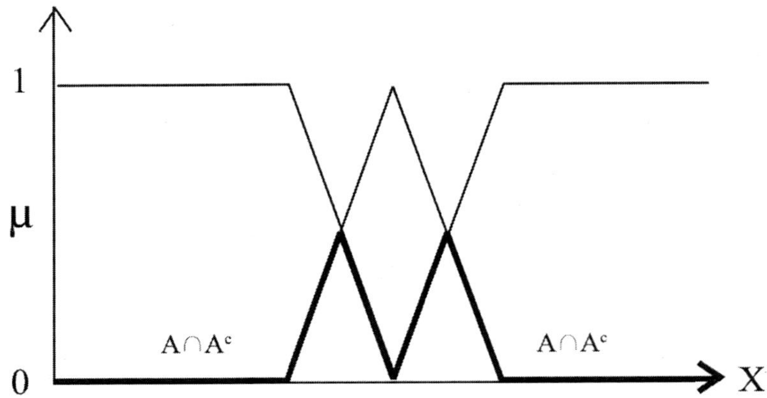


Figure 4.10. Fuzzy set $A \cap A^c \neq$ Empty set

Bart Kosko made use of this novel feature of fuzzy sets to formulate his fuzzy subsethood theorem which states that the whole set can also be contained in any of its subsets.[235] This is possible because, according to fuzzy set theory, fuzzy sets violate the law of complementarity in classical mathematics. The proof of the fuzzy subsethood theorem remains too complex for our purpose. Kosko's metaphor of cutting the tree illustrates his subsethood theorem.[236] The tree falls if you cut halfway through its trunk. This shows how the whole can be contained in the part.

The ideas of fuzzy containment and the fuzzy subsethood theorem (the whole set is contained in any of its subsets) help us to understand the Trinitarian paradox of "unity with distinction." Gregory and Basil addressed this paradox of "whole-part" relationship in the Trinity philosophically at two different

235 The fuzzy subsethood theorem was derived both algebraically and geometrically by Bart Kosko. He proved that the superset $A \cup A^c$ is a subset of its own subset $A \cap A^c$. This means the whole set can be contained in its own subset. For details, refer to Bart Kosko, "Fuzziness Vs Probability," *International Journal of General Systems*, vol. 17 (1990): 211-240. Also refer to Mamoni Dhar, "A Note on Subsethood Measure of Fuzzy Sets," *International Journal of Energy, Information and Communication*, vol. 3, no. 3, (2012): 55 and Zadeh, "Fuzzy Sets," 338-353. A mathematical demonstration of fuzzy subsethood theorem is given in the appendix.

236 Kosko, *Fuzzy Thinking*, 60.

levels (one at the level of ontology and the other at the level of epistemology) because they could not conceive how the whole could be contained in the part within a classical logical framework. Hence, they had to use philosophical categories of substance, particularities, power, causality, etc., to explain the unity at one level and distinction at another level, whereas fuzzy logic provides a single mathematical framework for both unity and distinction. In the fuzzy subsethood theorem, the whole remains "whole" and the part remains "part," while at the same time the "part" is fully contained in the "whole," and the "whole" can also be fully contained in the "part." The fuzzy subsethood theorem (the metaphor of cutting the tree) and the idea of fuzzy containment help us to comprehend the intra-Trinitarian unity and distinction both ontologically and epistemologically at the same level.

Fuzzy logic provides possibilities of full containment of the whole set in the part (extreme values) as well as partial containment (in degrees) at the same time. In this understanding, both Gregory's claim that there are no degrees in God as the whole is fully contained in the part, and Basil's claim that there is a certain order among the persons of the Trinity, as the part is contained in the whole, and the part remains part, and the whole remains whole, are reconciled simultaneously within a single fuzzy logical and critical realist framework. My conclusion is that more effectively than philosophy and classical mathematics, fuzzy logic offers a critical realist model and a critical way of thinking that provide a more rational basis for comprehending the Trinitarian paradox.

## 4.3 Fuzzy Logical Explanation of Religions' Claim to Uniqueness

The Indian context, to which I belong, is multi-religious. Religions, especially Christianity, struggle to reconcile their religious heritage and uniqueness claims (truth claims) of being the one, true or best religion with the apparent truth of other religions and faith traditions. Several scholars have attempted to reconcile this contradiction in diverse ways. In this section, I would like to explain the views of Paul F. Knitter, and employ a fuzzy logical explanation to further illuminate the possibilities.

### 4.3.1 Raimon Panikkar's *Cosmotheandric* Principle

Raimon Panikkar offers a cosmic understanding of religion designed to lead a change in attitude to other religions. Awareness of the universal theophany, that everything is ultimately unfolding to the ONE, provides a dynamic worldview which he calls *cosmotheandric* experience.[237] The term *cosmotheandric* denotes the intertwining of the "cosmic," the "human" and the "divine," all interpenetrating one another as different dimensions of the whole. The *cosmotheandric* experience enables one to enter into the hermeneutic circle of interrelatedness without which persons of different faith traditions cannot truly understand other religious families. The *cosmotheandric* principle suggests that the divine, the human and the earthly are three irreducible dimensions which constitute the reality. Panikkar emphasizes that the three dimensions of reality are neither three modes of a monolithic undifferentiated reality, nor three elements of a pluralistic system. Rather, though intrinsically threefold, relation manifests the ultimate constitution of reality. Everything that exists, any real being, presents this triune constitution expressed in three dimensions. Panikkar's principle provides a general worldview for making sense of every religious heritage on a relational platform, rooted in the interrelatedness of the cosmos, the divine and the human. However, he does not specifically address the uniqueness of truth claims in religions. Hence, we turn to Paul F. Knitter's four models for interreligious dialogue.

237 Raimon Panikkar, *The Cosmotheandric Experience* (Maryknoll, NY: Orbis Books, 1993), 8.

## 4.3.2 Paul F. Knitter's Four Models

While Panikkar offers a general relational approach to religions, Knitter presents four specific models of major theological positions on the relation of Christianity to other religions. They are the Total Replacement/ Partial Replacement Model, Fulfillment Model, Mutuality Model and Acceptance Model. The Replacement model holds that Christianity is meant to replace all other religions.[238] Fundamentalists and evangelicals are proponents of this model. In this theology, other religions have no value. It misses the very real presence of God within the world of other religions. According to the Partial Replacement Model, other religions have revelations but no salvation, because salvation is brought about by Jesus Christ and only by him.[239] Paul Tillich, Wolfhart Pannenberg and the New Evangelicals are representatives of this model. The Replacement Model, both full and partial, makes exclusivist claims. The Fulfillment Model represents a move from seeing Christianity as the replacement to the fulfillment of other religions.[240] In Knitter's opinion, theologians like Karl Rahner fall into this category. This model offers a theology that gives equal weight to the two foundational Christian convictions that God's love is universal, extending to all peoples, but also that God's love is particular, made real in Jesus Christ. This theology believes that other religions are of value, that God is to be found in them, that Christians need to dialogue with them and not just preach to them. However, it makes absolutist claims.

According to the Mutuality Model, there is only "one Real" but many cultural expressions.[241] John Hick is a prominent proponent of this model which attempts to balance the universality of God's revelation with the particularity of Jesus' revelation. The

---

238 Paul F. Knitter, *Introducing Theologies of Religions* (Maryknoll, NY: Orbis Books, 2002), 19.

239 Knitter, *Introducing Theologies of Religions*, 33.

240 Ibid., 63.

241 Ibid., 115.

supporters of this model affirm their claims using a philosophical-historical bridge which highlights the historical limitations of all religions and the philosophical possibility that there is one Divine Reality behind and within them all, the religious-mystical bridge which highlights the commonality of mystical experience in all religions, and the ethical-practical bridge which stresses the needs and suffering of humanity.[242] It is further substantiated through the use of the Kantian terminologies of *noumenon* (the Real) and *phenomenon* (diverse cultural expressions).

According to the Acceptance Model, the religious traditions of the world are different, so one needs to accept those differences. There are many religions and many salvations. George Lindbeck's post-liberal theology, Mark Heim's "Many salvations theology" and Francis X. Clooney's comparative theology represent this model. After considering the four models for theology of religions, Knitter concludes: "although we have a model of choice; we should not consider it as the only model or the absolute model." He means that "all the models have to check and balance--challenge and add to-- each other."[243]

Knitter's suggestion that there is no absolute model and his conclusion that "all the models have to check and balance--challenge and add to--each other" require further treatment. I will use fuzzy logic to verify it. To this end, I shall provide fuzzy logical explanation of truth.

### 4.3.3 Fuzzy Logical Explanation of Truth

We begin with the concept of truth. Philosophers distinguish logical truth from factual truth. Classical logical truth holds for statements that describe logical or mathematical truth. Either A or not A. In classical logic, 1 + 1 = 2. Truth in classical logic is represented by symbols and their formal relationships: Logical truths are necessary and are true in all cases. Logical falsehoods are false in all cases. Logical truth does not depend on how the world

242 Knitter, *Introducing Theologies of Religions*, 112-113.

243 Ibid., 242.

is and is not. Factual truths hold for statements that describe possible facts or events. Factual truths can be true in some cases and false in others. For example, "it is raining today." The truth of this statement depends on the context. So, factual truths are contingent.

Classical logical truth holds in possible worlds as the laws of logic and math hold in all worlds. Factual truths are true in some possible worlds, as physical laws may not hold everywhere. The split between logical truth and factual truth two corresponding theories of truth, the coherence theory and the correspondence theory. The statement 1 + 1 = 2 is true as we coherently apply the rule of math. Mathematics is a formal system. In a formal language statements are true if they obey the rules, or if they cohere with rules. The correspondence theory of truth assumes that a statement is true if it corresponds to fact. "The earth rotates" is true when the earth rotates. The statements correspond to or match events in time.

Scientific claims and statements are inexact and provisional as they depend on dozens of simplifying assumptions and axioms which are taken for granted. They build mathematical models to describe a little piece of the world or to describe the whole thing. Logical statements are completely accurate or completely inaccurate.[244] Factual statements are partially accurate and partially inaccurate. The logical and the factual do not meet. The danger is when scientists mix math with science. What is actually inaccurate is being bumped up into the true-or-false and all-or-none status of binary logic. Such a binary logical worldview is often held in religions too, leading to exclusive truth claims.

A Fuzzy logical explanation of truth differs from classical logical truth and factual truth. Fuzzy logic views truth as accuracy, where accuracy is clearly a matter of degree. Kosko differentiates the use of language (ways of communicating truth) in binary logic and fuzzy logic as follows:[245]

---

244 Kosko, *Fuzzy Thinking*, 86.

245 Ibid., 24.

| **Language of Binary Logic** | **Language of Fuzzy Logic** |
|---|---|
| Bivalence | Multivalence |
| A OR not-A | A AND not-A |
| Exact | Partial |
| All or none | Some degree |
| 0 or 1 | Continuum between 0 and 1 |
| Binary language | Fuzzy language |
| Bits | Fits |

The binary thinking and the fuzzy thinking are further differentiated diagrammatically as follows. Consider the figure given below (figure 4.11). Let the points $a_1$, $a_2$ denote the religions of Hinduism and Christianity along the horizontal axis, and $t_{a1}$ and $t_{a2}$ represent a Hindu and a Christian who belong to those respective religions along the vertical axis. In binary logical thinking, Hinduism and Christianity are understood as two single valued and separate points having no relation between two.

On the contrary, in fuzzy logical thinking, religion is not regarded as a single-valued number or point, but as a set. Let *a* and *b* be Hinduism and Christianity respectively along the horizontal axis, and let $t_a$ and $t_b$ be a Hindu and a Christian respectively along the vertical axis. Then $t_a$ and $t_b$ are represented as two fuzzy numbers or fuzzy persons, who can also have belongingness to another set at the same time, as shown in figure 4.12.

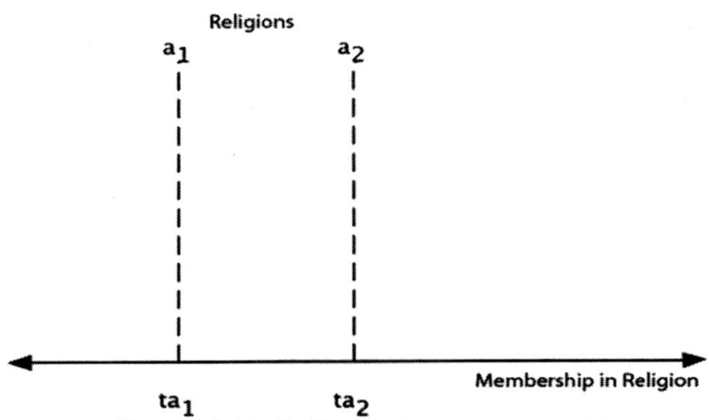


Figure 4.11. Religions as separate entities

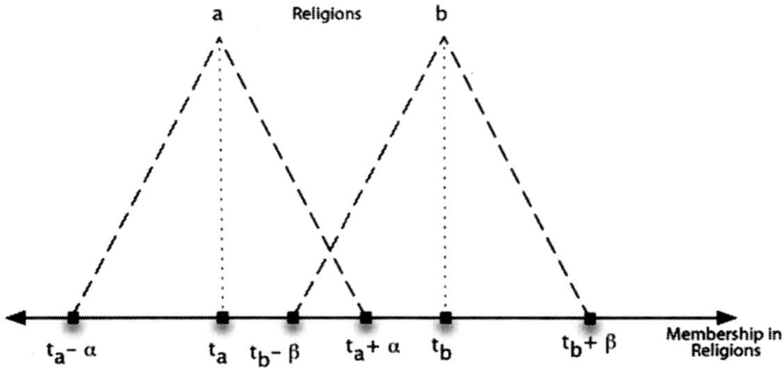


Figure 4.12. Religions as distinct entities

In the figure above, *a* and *b* are two distinct religions (Hinduism and Christianity) which are distinct, as $t_a$ is distinct from $t_b$. However, in fuzzy logic, unlike classical logic, $t_a$ and $t_b$ have durations respectively, because of their fuzzy membership function. All points between $t_a - \alpha$ and $t_a + \alpha$ belong to the fuzzy set of $t_a$ and similarly for $t_b$. The two durations of $t_a$ and $t_b$ share in common all points between $t_b - \beta$ and $t_a + \alpha$. Thus they are distinct but not separate. The same logic can be applied to other existing religions that all religions partially participate in one another.

Consider the same example above (figure 4.7) of a fuzzy set A, here say, which represents Christianity. The belongingness of each element *a*, *b*, *c* on the horizontal axis to the fuzzy set A of Christianity can be represented using membership values in the unit interval [0, 1] along the vertical axis.

As seen above, *a* belongs 100% to the fuzzy set A in the figure, and it belongs 0% to the complement of the fuzzy set A, denoted as $A^c$. Similarly, the degree of membership of the element *b* in fuzzy set A is denoted as $\mu_A(b) = 0.4$, which means that *b* belongs 40% to the fuzzy set A, and *b* belongs 60% to $A^c$. The degree of membership of the element *c* in fuzzy set A is denoted as $\mu_A(c) = 0$, which means that *c* does not belong to A at all, but *c* belongs 100% to $A^c$. Metaphorically when we treat A as the set of Christianity and $A^c$ as the set of non-Christian religions, then a Christian can be 100% Christian (membership in A) due to *a* as it belongs 100% to the fuzzy set A. *a* could be regarded as the hard core belief of a Christian in the Trinitarian God. Similarly, *b* and *c* having belongingness to other sets (having membership in non-A or $A^c$) open up the possibility of Christianity being open to other religions.

Fuzzy logic is non-classical logic. It differs from classical logic by the fundamental fact that it does not restrict the number of values of truth to only two: true or false (right or wrong). Fuzzy logic allows for a larger reference set of truth degrees. This means that fuzzy logic attributes the degree of membership of a statement to a set of trueness or falseness. This seemingly small difference in interpreting the degree of truth or falsehood leads to a fundamental divergence in the concept of truth. In fact, this difference results in a new way of thinking in which the concept of truth is dissociated from a universal definition. This means that, in this thinking, Christians can sensibly claim that Christ is unique; similarly, Hindus, Muslims, etc., can also make their uniqueness claims. This is often translated into relativity, however, in fuzzy thinking, it is the relativity of being true. Objective influences can only affect the truth of a phenomenon, not the entire concept of truth. This, again, means that finding and searching for the concept of truth is deemed to be a definite idea itself, but the concept's appearances (here, the concept of religion/truth claims) can alter from case to case, from time to time and from place to place, from religion to religion. This way of thinking (fuzzy thinking) accommodates various religions and their diverse truth claims. It provides religions an authentic basis for their uniqueness claims, but not for exclusive claims.

The language of fuzzy logic is both-and, as opposed to that of classical logic, which is either-or. The membership function in fuzzy logic is a matter of degree. Each element belongs to a set to a certain degree, varying between 0 and 1. Drawing an analogical parallel, the four models of Knitter can be placed on a fuzzy scale having degrees of membership. Thus, Fuzzy thinking substantiates Knitter's view that "there is no absolute model" and his conclusion that "all the models have to check and balance--challenge and add to--each other."

The 'both-and' paradigm (fuzzy paradigm) is holistic, comprised of interpersonal and transpersonal, anthropocentric and cosmo-centric, prophetic and mystic elements. The encounter with mystical traditions brings to our awareness that a religion without mystical depth is no religion at all. Coherent theological theories (creed), elaborate ritual performances (cult), detailed ethical norms (code), and people (community) cannot transform the lives of the people unless they are constantly nourished by the hidden streams of mystical experience. Christianity, deeply rooted in the Christ-experience, can be open to the power and presence of the Spirit manifest in other religions, in their sages and symbols, scriptures and traditions. In this process, Christians will be enriched by the word of God vibrant in other religions and transformed by the Spirit of God active in other religions.[246] The same will happen to the Hindus, the Muslims and people of other religious traditions. The new mission of religious in India is then to embrace the divine, the human and the cosmic in its fuller dimension. The truly religious person of the future will be an inter-religious person.

With a fuzzy logical explanation, in this section, I have made an attempt to understand religions' claim to uniqueness in a multi-religious context. It is shown that fuzzy thinking helps one to make sense of religions' claim to uniqueness.

## Conclusion

In this chapter, I have dealt with three applications of the study. In the first application, based on the works of Robert John Russell, I have provided a fuzzy logical framework for time and eternity to show how the distinction is maintained between events in eternity and the separation is overcome. In the second application, I have illustrated that better than philosophy and binary thinking,

246 S. Painadath SJ, *We are Co-Pilgrims* (Delhi: ISPCK, 2006), 22.

fuzzy logic/ fuzzy thinking can provide a critical realist thinking to address effectively the Trinitarian paradox of "unity with distinction." In the third application, I have shown that contrary to binary thinking, in fuzzy thinking religions can sensibly make their claims to uniqueness.

# 5. Fuzzy Thinking - Limitations and Possibilities

This chapter has two sections. The first section deals with the possibilities of fuzzy logic with reference to binary, relativist and probability thinking. The second section deals with the limitations of fuzzy logic and the fuzzy model of critical realism. The chapter ends by suggesting a few possibilities of exploring fuzzy thinking in religions and developing a fuzzy language for talking about God and religions in the multi-religious and multi-cultural context of India.

## 5.1 Fuzzy Thinking beyond Binary and Relativist Thinking

Modern dualistic traditions have been more critical of fuzzy logic than postmodern relativist thinking. In 1972, Professor Emil Rudolf Kalman responded to Zadeh's talk on fuzzy sets and systems at the Man and Computer Conference in Bordeaux, France: "No doubt Professor Zadeh's enthusiasm for fuzziness has been reinforced by the prevailing political climate in the U.S.--one of unprecedented permissiveness. 'Fuzzification' is a kind of scientific permissiveness; it tends to result in socially appealing slogans unaccompanied by the discipline of hard scientific work and patient observation."[247] In 1975, a reporter summarized Zadeh's position as follows:

> 'Fuzzy theory is wrong, wrong and pernicious,' says William Kahman, a professor of computer sciences and mathematics at Cal [University of California, Berkeley] whose Evans Hall office is a few doors down from Zadeh's. 'I cannot think of any problem that could not be solved better by ordinary logic....What Zadeh is saying is the same sort of things as 'Technology got us into this mess and now it can't get us out.' Well, technology did not get us into this mess. Greed and weakness and ambivalence got us into this mess. What we need is more logical thinking, not less. The danger of fuzzy logic is that it will encourage the sort of imprecise thinking that has bought us so much trouble.'[248]

These criticisms emerge from binary thinking based on Aristotle's logic which ensures that every well-formed statement is either true or false. This way of thinking divides the realities of the world into a "yes or no" paradigm. There is no possibility of being in-between. Most often, binary-valued thinking runs through our language and thought patterns.[249] In our daily life, thinking and language cannot be restricted to two-valued logic, as there is always a need for something beyond binary thinking. For example, in binary thinking, a person may be assessed as either brilliant or not brilliant. That means a person must belong to one set or the other. Partial set membership is considered impossible. In the example of assessing someone as brilliant, views that admit someone to be very brilliant, more or less brilliant, almost

247 Rudolf E. Kalman is a Hungarian-American electrical engineer who designed the "Kalman filter," used more than any other system in navigation, guidance, estimation, and in hundreds of other computer tasks. Daniel McNeill and Paul Freiberger, *Fuzzy Logic* (New York: Simon & Schuster, 1993), 46.

248 Cited in McNeill and Freiberger, *Fuzzy Logic*, 47.

249 Priyanka, "Relevancy of Fuzzy Concept in Mathematics," 312.

brilliant, not very brilliant, etc., are not tolerated, whereby the subjective factors of reasoning are often sidelined. However, fuzzy logic admits subjective factors like more or less, almost, very, not very, etc. This expresses our mind and life more adequately.[250]

Fuzzy logic allows partial set membership such that a member can be a member of a given set in part and, at the same time, not. While traditional binary thinking recognizes either full membership or none, fuzzy thinking allows partial truth and partial falseness. Unlike binary thinking, fuzzy logic takes into account intermediate truth values along with the absolutes. Thus, fuzzy thinking can strike a balance between the binary world view of modernity and the relative worldview of postmodernity by retaining its mathematical foundations while emphasizing its intermediate truth-values.

## 5.2 Fuzzy Thinking beyond Probability Thinking

Fuzzy thinking also invites criticism from the probability school of statistics. Zadeh uses numbers in the unit interval [0, 1] to describe truth as matter of degree. Probability theorists think they apply the same approach, using the unit interval, in dealing with randomness. For example, probability of the occurrence of an event may vary from 0 to 1.

Most often statisticians/probability theorists equate fuzziness with randomness. But for Zadeh, fuzziness and randomness differ both at the levels of concept and theory. Randomness involves uncertainty in the outcome (random experiment) but fuzziness involves uncertainty in the meaning of data. In other words, randomness describes the uncertainty of the occurrence of an event whereas, fuzziness describes the ambiguity of the event itself.

While probabilistic methods are efficient tools to better deal with randomness, the fuzzy logical method (the use of fuzzy sets, membership functions and the method of defuzzification, etc.) helps to appropriately tackle fuzziness. Probability and fuzzy sets

250 Ibid., 311.

deal with different kinds of uncertainty. As the probability theory makes a prediction or expectation of a future event based on some prior known facts, the sense of uncertainty revolves around this process. On the contrary, the sense of fuzziness is related to the uncertainty resulting from the imprecision of meaning of an event. Most of the human decisions rely on propositions that deal with the meaning of event occurrence, not just the occurrence of an event. Probability theory by itself is inadequate to deal with uncertainty at the meaning level.[251] To improve its efficiency, probability theory needs to draw concepts and techniques from fuzzy logic. For example, the fuzzy random variables in statistics combine both randomness and fuzziness to deal with both the meaning and the occurrence of an event.

In spite of these tremendous prospects and possibilities over and beyond binary thinking, relativist thinking and probability thinking, fuzzy logic has its limitations. In the next section, I shall explain the limitations and possibilities of fuzzy logic and the fuzzy model of critical realism in detail.

## 5.3 Fuzzy Logic: Limitations and Possibilities

To assess the limitations of fuzzy logic, I find Susan Haack's works useful. A professor of philosophy and law at the University of Miami in the United States, Haack critiques Zadeh's fuzzy thinking for methodological limitations, truth-value complexities and linguistic incorrectness. According to Haack, Zadeh seems to rely on two main preferences: a methodological preference to avoid the complexities inevitably introduced by the regimentation of informal argument; and a linguistic preference to acknowledge "true" and "false" as fuzzy predicates which are not precise.[252]

In explaining the methodological limitations, Haack claims that fuzzy logic does not avoid the complexities introduced by

251 T. Pathi Nathan, "In Search of Truth through Uncertainty Paradigm," *Convergence*, vol. 1 (2004): 11-12.

252 Susan Haack, *Deviant Logic, Fuzzy Logic: Beyond the Formalism* (London: The University of Chicago Press, 1996), 238.

regimentation. For Zadeh, fuzzy logic can directly represent informal arguments, vague premises and/or conclusions, and thus avoids the need to regiment them. But for Haack, Zadeh's claim is misleading, as two kinds of argument may affect the predicates used in an argument: unidimensional (having only one relevant variable, e.g. beautiful or tall. To be tall one should be fairly tall).[253] The regimentation of unidimensional vagueness results in artificiality. The regimentation of multidimensional vagueness results in complexity. Haack observes,

> Fuzzy logic indeed avoids the need to regiment unidimensional vagueness—one can assign a fuzzy set to "tall," instead of setting down an arbitrary cut-off point. But it does not avoid the need to regiment unidimensional vagueness; and yet it is here that regimentation introduces complexities. Zadeh claims that fuzzy logic can handle multidimensional as well as unidimensional vagueness, but this claim is quite misleading, as one can see by looking closely at his detailed diagnoses of predicates with multidimensional vagueness. What Zadeh does is first to analyze such predicates into weighted components in a purely intuitive way, and then to introduce the apparatus of fuzzy logic to deal with any residual unidimensional vagueness in the components. The formal apparatus is almost wholly redundant; the real work is done at the level of informal linguistic analysis.[254]

Haack claims that fuzzy logic introduces enormous complexities. Zadeh regards fuzzy truth values as much more appropriate than numerical truth values. But in Haack's view, to take as truth-values all fuzzy subsets of [0, 1] would be "much too rich and much too difficult to manipulate," thus leading

---

253 Ibid., 238.

254 Ibid.

to fearsome complexities.[255] She notes that fuzzy logic imposes artificial precision. It only postpones and does not eliminate the need to introduce arbitrary boundaries. Haack explains:

> At the level of the base logics, though one is not obliged to require that a predicate either definitely applies or definitely does not apply, one is obliged to require that a predicate definitely apply to such-and-such, rather than to such-and-such other degree [e.g. that a man 5' 10" in tall belongs to *tall* to degree 0.6 rather than 0.5]. And at the second level of fuzzification, one has arbitrarily to fix the degree to which a given numerical true-value should belong to the linguistic truth-value *true*, and to define the operators *very, not,* and so forth.[256]

In Haack's view, fuzzy logic also suffers from linguistic incorrectness. She argues that the view of truth on which the motivation for fuzzy logic relies is mistaken. Zadeh's claim that truth is a matter of degree rests on the thesis that the adverbial modifiers that apply to "true" are those which typically apply to fuzzy predicates. According to Haack, Zadeh is mistaken in his use of this linguistic evidence. For example, she writes:

There are certain adverbs among them [adverbial modifiers] 'quite' and 'very,' which apply both to predicates like 'tall,' 'old,' etc., and to 'true' and 'false.' When applied to what I shall call 'predicates of degree,' i.e., predicates denoting properties that come in degrees, 'quite' and 'very' typically indicate possession of the property in, respectively, modest or considerable degree. Zadeh, observes that 'quite true' indicates the possession of a modest degree of truth, and 'very true' the possession of a high degree of truth.[257]

---

255 Haack, *Deviant Logic, Fuzzy Logic: Beyond the Formalism*, 239.

256 Ibid.

257 Ibid., 240.

Haack claims that this cannot be right. She illustrates with the following example. 'Quite tall' can be roughly equated with 'rather tall,' but 'quite true' cannot be equated with 'rather true' or fairly true.' In fact, various adverbs which typically modify predicates of degree do not apply to 'true' at all.

Apart from methodological limitations, truth-value complexities and linguistic incorrectness, other limitations apply as well. Esko Turunen, associate professor of logic at Tampere University of Technology, Finland, asks whether fuzzy logic is complete from a mathematical point of view. In mathematics, there are two forms of completeness: axiomatic and semantic.[258] Turunen derives a semantic completeness theorem for fuzzy logic. He says, "Any consistent fuzzy theory *T* is semantically complete."[259] However, Turnen acknowledges that fuzzy theories are not axiomatizable even within a semantically complete system, which leads him to formulate an incompleteness theorem for fuzzy logic that fuzzy logic is axiomatically incomplete.

Fuzzy logic invites practical difficulties at the application level. How can degree of membership be applied to concrete possibilities? For example, suppose somebody applies fuzzy categories to a fetus, its degree of membership in the human class could be 0 at conception, gradually increase as time passes, and reach 1 at the time of birth. Similarly, an old person's degree of membership in the human class could be regarded as decreasing as one continues to age. What about the degree of membership for a handicapped person in the set of human classifications? Fuzzy logic and fuzzy technology could be misused. To prevent misuse, fuzzy claims and fuzzy explanations need to be precise

258 A mathematical system is axiomatically complete if a true proposition can be proved within that system. For details, refer to Michat Walicki, *Introduction to Mathematical Logic* (Singapore: World Scientific, 2012), 35-36.

259 Esko Turunen, *Mathematics Behind Fuzzy Logic* (Heidelberg: Physica-verlag, 1999), 98.

and clear. One must be vigilant in not using fuzzy logic to make counterproductive decisions in life.[260]

In spite of these limitations mentioned above, fuzzy logic is advantageous in real life compared to the classical mathematical approach. Control systems can be described more accurately using fuzzy logic than with traditional mathematics. Fuzzy logic is widely used in artificial intelligence, computer science and robotics, as well as in many other forms of hardware and software in use today.[261] As fuzzy logic excels in dealing with imprecision, it serves as a powerful mathematical tool for modeling and simulating uncertain systems in nature, in science, industry and business. Other applications of fuzzy systems theory and fuzzy-logic controllers include information retrieval systems, navigation systems for automatic vehicles, water level controllers in laboratories, feature-definition controllers for robot vision, graphics controllers for automated police sketchers, financial planners, decision-support systems in government policies, diagnostic systems in medical science and meteorology.[262]

## 5.4 Fuzzy Model of Critical Realism: Limitations and Possibilities

I have used the fuzzy model of critical realism to improve upon modern and postmodern explanations of critical realism as well as to draw a fuzzy framework for the science-theology dialogue. Does a fuzzy model of critical realism take into account every nuance of modernity and postmodernity? The nuances of modernity and postmodernity are diverse, numerous and variously explained. Hence, it is important to acknowledge that I have used the terms postmodern and modern in ways different from standard usage.

The turn to modernity in the writings of Immanuel Kant distinguished the modality of apprehension of the *phenomenon* and the *noumenon,* whereby the former was apprehended and

260 McNeill and Freiberger, *Fuzzy Logic*, 13.

261 Priyanka, "Relevancy of Fuzzy Concept in Mathematics," 312.

262 Ibid., 315.

interpreted by pure reason, while the latter was epistemologically inaccessible. Whereas Aquinas' notion of reason comprehended different functions, but the same reason was involved in the perception of the natural and moral order, Kant distinguishes different rational faculties in the individual, so that the laws of nature are the purview of pure reason, and the laws of morality are the purview of practical reason. Postmodernity, in this perspective, appears to be an intensification of modernity, where the epistemological inaccessibility of the *noumenon* becomes *de facto* a claim about its ontological non-existence. Derrida discussed this as the perpetual sliding of the signified under the signifier. Language absorbs everything and is all encompassing (a kind of flight from ontology).

Modernity postulates the possibility of grasping the truth of reality partially (though not totally as in the traditional forms of Thomist realism). Postmodernity challenges that entirely (it would seem that there is no reality). My fuzzy model of critical realism appears to use the terms modernity and postmodernity in ways different from the standard, and it asserts the possible coexistence of a modern and a postmodern approach. To be precise, in my study, the fuzzy model of critical realism focusses only on overcoming the binary thinking. Fuzzy thinking appears to accommodate modernity without indulging in reductionism and postmodernism without indulging in relativism.

I have demonstrated a fuzzy framework to enhance the science-theology dialogue (figure 4.8). The framework, in general, accommodates crisp events along the horizontal axis and fuzzy events along the vertical axis. The graph can take up only those axes referring to epistemology (crisp and fuzzy). The ontological representation of events remains vague even though the ontological existence of events is acknowledged. The same limitation is faced while providing a fuzzy logical framework for time and eternity. The ontological representations of resurrection, New Creation and eternity are placed on a hyperbolic curve in an act of faith, which cannot be proved mathematically. Similarly, the dimension of mystery still remains while attempting to understand the Trinitarian paradox using fuzzy thinking. The application of fuzzy thinking in religions also suffers from limitations as relativist thinking may creep in if the fuzzy worldview is not understood properly.

Do we need fuzzy model of critical realism? In spite of its limitations, fuzzy logic and the fuzzy model of critical realism still remain promising for science-theology dialogue. The experience of limit in the fuzzy model must be an inspiration to explore further the ontological and epistemological mysteries of our life. Although, a fuzzy logical approach may not offer a one-off remedy to any question that arises during the methodological bridging between science and theology, instead, this approach devises an open-ended decision tool that can continue to improve as time goes on and as circumstances change. The theory of fuzzy logic and the fuzzy model of critical realism provide a mathematical basis for comprehending the uncertainties and ambiguities associated with the human cognitive processes of thinking and reasoning both in science and theology. As a result, fuzzy thinking provides an adequate conceptual framework for science and theology to engage in dialogue and to address the complex realities of human life.

I find fuzzy thinking highly promising in the multi-religious and multicultural context of India to promote interreligious dialogue. I have explained how fuzzy thinking substantiates people of different religions making unique truth claims. In a fuzzy worldview, distinctions between religions are maintained and separation between religions is overcome. Fuzzy thinking can be helpful in understanding the diverse schools of Indian religions and their philosophies. For example, the Hindu Scriptures talk about *Aham Brhmasmi* – "I'm *Brahman*" (*Brhadaranyaka Upanishad* 1.4.10 of the *Yajur Veda*) and *Tat Tvam Asi* -- "Thou art That" (*Chandogya Upanishad* 6.8.7 of the *Sama Veda*). In binary thinking, God, the cosmos and the humans are separate, whereas, in fuzzy thinking they are interrelated, as it provides a frame of thought which entails a single act of knowing. This leads to the possibility of developing a fuzzy language for talking about God and religions.

Fuzzy thinking is useful in appreciating fuzzy concepts in Buddhist thinking. For example, the concept of *Shunyata* in Buddhism sounds fuzzy. The ultimate reality for Buddhism is *Shunyata.*[263] Its literal meaning is vacuum, emptiness, void or absolute nothingness. It is unobjectifiable and non-conceptualizable. There is no dominant – subordinate relationship and no subject – object relationship in *Shunyata*. Everything is dominant over everything else and at the same time everything is subordinate to everything else.[264] There is interpenetration and mutual reversibility in *Shunyata*, including all the opposites. In *Shunyata*, reality is a non-dual continuum. The absolute and phenomenological are perspectives or aspects and not separate ontological realms. *Shunyata* is oneness in differentiation. It is the unified awareness that comprehends and transcends both oneness and differentiation. *Shunyata* seems meaningless in binary thinking, but meaningful in fuzzy thinking.

Fuzzy thinking functions in Jainism too as Jainism offers a doctrine called *Anekantavada*, the principles of pluralism and multiplicity of viewpoints. This implies that the concepts of truth and reality are perceived differently from different points of view, and that no single point of view is the complete truth. This doctrine encourages its proponents to consider the views and beliefs of one's rivals and opposing parties in order to overcome one's own limited views. This principle influenced Mahatma Gandhi in adopting principles of religious tolerance, *ahimsa* (non-violence) and *Satyagraha* (insistence on truth). It is interesting that Jains developed a logic out of this doctrine,

---

263 Masao Abe, "Kenosis and Emptiness," in *Buddhist Emptiness and Christian Trinity*, ed., Roger Corless and Paul F. Knitter (Mahwa, NJ: Paulist Press, 1990), 20.

264 Abe, "Kenosis and Emptiness," 21.

namely *Syādvāda* (logic on *perhaps*). The underlying principle of this logic is that no single proposition can express the nature of reality fully.

In general, fuzzy thinking helps us to understand appreciate the profound notion of fuzziness. It can be further used as an interpretative (hermeneutical) category for religious language. Such an attempt will enable us to understand better God and religions.

The aim of my study is to foster science-theology dialogue. The study, in particular, has focused on the methodological bridging between science and theology with reference to critical realism. In this work, I defined critical realism within a fuzzy logical framework. I argued that a fuzzy model of critical realism would help to overcome the nuances of binary thinking without indulging in reductionism or relativism by adding more levels of intermediate truth values to the idea of absolutes. I also argued that this model offers an inclusive epistemological framework for science-theology dialogue where multiple referential claims reinforce one another. I demonstrated, with the help of a two-dimensional (2D) coordinate system, how the fuzzy model of critical realism enhances science-theology dialogue within a single critical realist, fuzzy framework. In this model, the correspondence theory of truth was not replaced but complemented by a coherence version of truth. Reference to the external or objective world was retained, while subjective constructivism was acknowledged integral to it in a single act of human knowing.

# Epilogue

We have discussed a framework based on fuzzy logical thinking for bridging mathematics (fuzzy logic), philosophy (critical realism) and theology (Eternity and Trinity). It is shown that a fuzzy model of critical realism helps to overcome the nuances of binary thinking without indulging in reductionism or relativism. It is also brought to light that this model provides an inclusive epistemological framework for science-theology dialogue. Mathematics (fuzzy logic) is used as a tool to explain philosophical and theological concepts and terminologies.

Logic is the art of arriving at conclusions from a set of premises. It is the skill of correct reasoning. Logic can be put into a formal language. The formal language consists of a series of signs and rules of syntax. While mathematics includes logic, it cannot be reduced to formal logic. Because mathematics has something more like axioms which are based on mathematical intuition. There is a one to one correspondence between mathematics and logic as realized through the set theory and the propositional calculus. This can be understood in terms of a parallelism between concepts and operations used in the two schemes. For example, the concept of set in mathematics and the concept of proposition in logic correspond with each other. Fuzzy logic is a precise mathematical tool which deals with uncertain and fuzzy situations.

Validity, soundness, completeness, and consistency are properties of any logical system. An argument is said to be valid in logic, if and only if it takes a form that makes it impossible for the premises to be true and the conclusion false. A logical statement is sound if it is valid and the premises are actually true. Consistency means that no two theorems within a system can contradict one another. It implies that all true propositions can be proved within the system. Completeness means there are no true propositions which cannot be proved in the system implying that only true propositions can be proven within the system.

A mathematical or logical system may or may not be complete. For example, according to Gödel's theorems, the first order predicate logic is complete, while an axiomatic formalized consistent system may be incomplete. In contrast with mathematics/logic, a scientific theory is necessarily incomplete. The historical trajectory of the development of science provides adequate evidence for this. Till the sixteenth century, the scientific world upheld the Aristotelian metaphysical worldview, which defined the beings of the universe on the basis of substance and accidents. Aristotle proposed a static worldview, presupposing a divinely designed natural order behind every phenomenon. Even the seventeenth and eighteenth century developments could not make a fundamental change to the static world-view of the scientific realm. The Helio-centric model of Nicholas Copernicus, the theories of Galileo Galilei, the planetary laws of Johannes Kepler, and the laws of motion of Isaac Newton further emphasized a mechanized world-view. Such mechanization meant that science could give us absolute accuracy, absolute certainty and exact predictability. The universe was considered deterministic. This also meant that scientific knowledge was perfectly objective, rational and exact. However the developments in science in the nineteenth and twentieth centuries like the theory of evolution, the theory of relativity, the Big Bang theory, the chaos theory and the quantum mechanics made the scientific world more dynamic. In the light of the developments in contemporary science (physical, biological and cosmological) we may come to the conclusion that uncertainties and contingencies are part and parcel of the scientific world.

Philosophy is the study of the basic nature of knowledge, reality and existence. Philosophy can be considered as a primitive form of mathematics (logic) and science. Philosophers make observations, indulge in reflections, and draw conclusions. However philosophy should not be equated with mathematics or science because it is neither as rigorous as mathematics nor as reliable as science. Mathematics is a formal activity based on well defined rules applicable to a set of symbols. This means, mathematics refers primarily to objects of the mind, while in science, there is also a reference to the external world in terms of phenomena. It means that the natural science refers to objects of our sense experience. Neither science nor mathematics talks about the ultimate causes. To this, we need to use the language of philosophy or theology or religion.

A scientific theory deals with the realities of nature. Religion/ theology is concerned with God. Religion refers to a particular system of belief or worship. In general, the code (law), the creed (faith proclamation), the cult (rites and rituals) and the community (faithful) constitute a religion. Theology is the systematic study of the nature of God and belief in God.

All the domains mentioned above are not water-tight compartments; but there are interconnections among them. The inter-relationships between different departments of enquiry are not well defined. In other words, there is fuzziness in appropriating these domains. This is the principal argument of this book. It means that none of these areas of knowledge can claim to be the purveyor of absolute truth. We need insights from all of them in order to arrive at a sensible and coherent worldview.

# Appendix
# Fuzzy Subsethood Theorem

In this section, I will be highlighting, in general, the mathematical representation of the fuzzy subsethood theorem and its related terminologies to get us familiarized with the theorem. A detailed proof is beyond the scope of this study as they can be traced in the original works by Bart Kosko.[1] The fuzzy subsethood theorem was derived both algebraically and geometrically by Kosko. Given two fuzzy sets A and B, it defines the degree to which one set belongs to another and is expressed by the formula.[2]

$$S(A, B) = \frac{M\ A \cap B}{M(A)}$$

where M (A) represents the fuzzy cardinality of fuzzy set A. In fuzzy mathematics, the cardinality of fuzzy sets is a measure of the number of the elements belonging to the set.[3] According to Mamoni Dhar:

> Analogous to the cardinal theory of sets, there are two approaches to the Cardinal theory of fuzzy sets-one of which is the fuzzy cardinality of fuzzy sets and the other which uses ordinary cardinal, ordinary numbers or real numbers or some generalization of ordinary numbers of cardinal numbers. In the first approach, since the results based on comparison of two fuzzy sets are rather

theoretical than practical, the main attention to the fuzzy cardinal theory was focused on the second approach.[4]

In scalar approaches, the cardinalities of fuzzy sets are defined by mapping where a single ordinary cardinal number or a non-negative real number is assigned to each fuzzy set. Accordingly, the scalar cardinality of fuzzy set A: $\Omega \rightarrow [0, 1]$ is defined as the sum of the membership degrees of finite fuzzy set A. That is symbolically defined as[5]

$$|A| = \sum_{x\varepsilon\Omega} A(X)$$

Since an element can partially belong to a fuzzy set a natural generalization of the classical notion of cardinality is to weigh each element by its membership degree. Then the formula for cardinality of a fuzzy set is defined as:[6]

$$|A| = \Sigma\mu_A(x), \text{ for all } x\varepsilon\Omega,$$

Where | A | is called the sigma-count of A (denoted by $\Sigma$ Count).

Then the fuzzy subsethood can be further defined by the formula:[7]

$$S(A, B) = \frac{\{|A| - \Sigma\max\{0, A(X) - B(C)))}{|A|}$$

Kosko introduced a non-probabilistic entropy measure in fuzzy sets and showed that the fuzzy entropy measure of a fuzzy set is the degree to which $A \cup A^c$ is a subset of $A \cap A^c$.[8] The following expression was proposed to relate subsethood measure with fuzzy entropy:[9]

$$R_1(P) = S(A\cup A^c, A\cap A^c), \text{ where } R_1(P) = \frac{\Sigma\text{Count}(A\cap A^c)}{\Sigma\text{Count}(A\cup A^c)}$$

$$S(A, B) = \frac{\Sigma\text{Count}(A\cap A^c)}{\Sigma\text{Count}(A\cup A^c)} \text{ and}$$

$S(A\cup A^c, A\cap A^c)$ measures the degree of subsethood of $A\cup A^c$ in $A\cap A^c$, and $A^c$ is the complement of the fuzzy set A, the membership function of which is considered as one minus the membership function of the fuzzy set A. With non-fuzzy sets $A \cap A^c$ is empty and so the numerator equals zero. But with fuzzy sets, the intersection is not empty, so there is overlap, and the numerator is always greater than zero. In other words, $R_1(P)$ represents the degree to which the superset $A \cup A^c$ is a subset of its own subset $A \cap A^c$. So using the formula of subsethood we show that the universe of discourse is also contained in any of its subsets. This is possible because according to the fuzzy set theory the fuzzy sets violate the two basic properties of crisp sets, the law of contradiction and the law of excluded middle.

## Endnotes

1 Bart Kosko, "Fuzziness Vs Probability," *International Journal of General Systems*, vol. 17 (1990): 211-240.
2 Kosko, "Fuzziness Vs Probability," 232.
3 Mamoni Dhar, "Cardinality of Fuzzy Sets: An Overview," *International Journal of Energy, Information and Communications*, vol. 4, no.1, 15-22, (2013), 15.
4 Dhar, "Cardinality of Fuzzy Sets: An Overview," 15.
5 Ibid., 16.
6 Ibid.
7 Mamoni Dhar, "A Note on Subsethood Measure of Fuzzy Sets," *International Journal of Energy, Information and Communication*, vol. 3, no. 3, 55-62 (2012), 55.
8 Entropy is regarded as a measure of fuzziness in fuzzy sets. Entropy means the uncertainty or disorder in a system. A set describes a system or collection of things. When the set is fuzzy, when elements belong to it to some degree, the set is uncertain or vague to some degree. Fuzzy entropy measures this degree. For details, refer to Zadeh, "Fuzzy Sets," 338-353.
9 Bart Kosko, "Entropy and Conditioning," *Information Sciences*, vol. 40 (1986): 165-174, 168 & 171.

# Bibliography

Abe, Masao. "Kenosis and Emptiness." In *Buddhist Emptiness and Christian Trinity*, ed. Roger Corless and Paul F. Knitter: 5-25. Mahwa, NJ: Paulist Press, 1990.

Ayres, Lewis. *Nicea and Its Legacy: An Approach to Fourth Century Trinitarian Theology*. Oxford: Oxford University Press, 2004.

Barbour, Ian G. *Issues in Science and Religion*. Englewood Cliffs, NJ: Prentice Hall, 1966.

________. *Issues in Science and Religion*. San Francisco: Harper & Row, 1966.

________. *Myths, Models, and Paradigms: A Comparative Study in Science and Religion*. San Francisco: Harper & Row, 1974.

________. *Religion and Science: Historical and Contemporary Issues*. San Francisco: Harper, 1997.

________. *Religion in an Age of Science*. Gifford Lectures; 1989-1991. Vol. 1. New York: Harper, 1990.

Barnes, Barry. *Interests and the Growth of Knowledge*. London: Routledge & Kegan Paul, 1977.

Bhaskar, Roy. *A Realist Theory of* Science. 2nd edition. London: Routledge, 2008.

________. *Dialectic: The Pulse of Freedom*. 2nd edition. London: Routledge, 2008.

________. "General Introduction." In *Critical Realism: Essential Readings*, ed. Margaret Archer, Roy Bhaskar, Andrew Collier,

Tony Lawson and Alan Norrie: ix-xxiv. London: Routledge, 1998.

________. *The Possibility of Naturalism.* 3rd edition. London: Routledge, 1998.

Bloor, David. *Knowledge and Social Imagery.* 2nd edition. Chicago: The University of Chicago Press, 1991.

Cat, Jordi. "Philosophical Perspectives on Fuzzy Set-Theoretical Models of Causality." In *Causality: Metaphysics and Methods, Technical Report 19/04*, ed. Julian Reiss: 1-12. London: London School of Economics, 2004.

Clayton, Philip. "Shaping the Field of Theology and Science: A Critique of Nancey Murphy." *Zygon.* Vol. 34, no. 4 (1999): 598-618.

________. *Explanation from Physics to Theology: An Essay in Rationality and Religion.* New Haven, CT: Yale University Press, 1989.

Colyvan, Mark. *An Introduction to the Philosophy of Mathematics.* Cambridge: Cambridge University Press, 2012.

Congar, Yves. *I Believe in the Holy Spirit: Volume III.* Trans. David Smith. New York: The Seabury Press, 1980.

Davies, Paul. *The Mind of God: The Scientific Basis for a Rational World.* New York: Simon and Schuster, 1992.

Derrida, Jacques. *Of Grammatology.* Trans. Gayatri Chakravorty Spivak. Baltimore: Johns Hopkins University Press, 1976.

Dhar, Mamoni. "A Note on Subsethood Measure of Fuzzy Sets."*International Journal of Energy, Information and Communication.* Vol. 3, no. 3 (2012): 55-61.

Drake, Durant. *Essay in Critical Realism: A Co-operative Study of the Problem of Knowledge.* London: Macmillan, 1920.

Einstein, Albert. *Out of My Later Years.* New York: Philosophical Library, 1950.

Erickson, Millard J. *Evangelical Interpretation.* Grand Rapids: Baker, 1993.

Fortman, Edmund J. *The Triune God.* Philadelphia: Westminster Press, 1972.

Foucault, Michel. "Truth and Power." In *Power/Knowledge: Selected Interviews and Other Writings, 1972-1977*, ed. Colin Gordon: 109-133. New York: Pantheon, 1980.

Fuller, Robert. *Fuzzy Reasoning and Fuzzy Optimization*. Turku, Finland: University of Turku and Abo Academy, 1998.

Gadamer, Hans-Georg. *Truth and Method*. Trans. Garret Barden and John Cumming. New York: Crossroad, 1984.

Ghomshei, Mori M., John A. Meech and Reza Naderi. "Fuzzy Logic in a Postmodern Era." Paper presented at Berkeley Initiative in Soft Computing (BISC) special event in honor of Professor Lotfi A. Zadeh at the University of California, Berkeley, Nov. 2-5 (2005).

Grenz, Stanley J. "Star Trek and the Next generation: Postmodernism and the Future of Evangelical Theology." In *The Challenge of Postmodernism: An Evangelical Engagement*, ed. David S. Dockery: 89-103. Grand Rapids, MI: Bakers Books, 1995.

Griffin, David Ray. *Varieties of Postmodern Theology*. Albany, NY: State University of New York, 1989.

Haack, Susan. *Deviant Logic, Fuzzy Logic: Beyond the Formalism*. London: The University of Chicago Press, 1996.

Hawking, Stephen and Leonard Mlodinow. *The Grand Design*. New York: Bantam Books, 2010.

John P. Leavey, "Four Protocols: Derrida, His Deconstruction," *Semeia*. Vol. 23 (1982): 42-57.

Karuvelil, George. "Pragmatism, Existentialism, and Media Theory as Approaches to Religion and Science." *Zygon*. Vol. 47, no. 2 (2012): 415-437.

Kaushal, Priyanka, Neeraj Mohan and Parvinder S. Sandhu. "Relevancy of Fuzzy Concept in Mathematics."*International Journal of Innovation: Management and Technology*. Vol. 1, no. 3 (2010): 312-315.

Kelsey, David. *The Use of Scripture in Recent Theology*. Philadelphia: Fortress Press, 1975.

Klein, Abbe Felix. *The Doctrine of the Trinity.* Trans. Daniel J. Sullivan. New York: P.J. Kennedy and Sons, 1940.

Knitter, Paul F. *Introducing Theologies of Religions.* Maryknoll, NY: Orbis Books, 2002.

Kosko, Bart. *Fuzzy Thinking: The New Science of Fuzzy Logic.* New York: Hyperion, 1993.

Kozhamthadam, Job. "The Changing Face of Science-Christianity Dialogue: Encouragement, Estrangement, and Engagement." In *Science, Technology and Values,* ed. Job Kozhamthadam: 3-34.Pune, India: ASSR Publications, 2003.

Kuhn, Thomas. *The Structure of Scientific Revolutions.* 2nd edition. Chicago: University of Chicago Press, 1987.

Lakatos, Imre. *The Methodology of Scientific Research Programs.* Cambridge: Cambridge University Press, 1978.

Leach, Javier. *Mathematics and Religion: Our Languages of Sign and Symbol.* Pennsylvania:Templeton Press, 2010.

Li, Zhong. *Fuzzy Chaotic Systems: Modeling, Control, and Applications.* Berlin: Germany, Springer-Verlag, 2006.

MacIntyre, Alasdair. "Epistemological Crises, Dramatic Narrative, and the Philosophy of Science," *Monist.* Vol. 60 (1977): 453-72.

McFague, Sallie. *Metaphorical Theology: Models of God in Religious Language.* Philadelphia: Fortress Press, 1982.

_________. *A Scientific Theology: Reality.* Vol. 2. Grand Rapids, MI: William B. Eerdmans Publishing Co., 2002.

McMullin, Ernan. "How Should Cosmology Relate to Theology?" In *The Sciences and Technology in the Twentieth Century,* ed. Arthur R. Peacocke: 17-57. Notre Dame, IN: University of Notre Dame Press, 1981.

McNeill, Daniel and Paul Freiberger. *Fuzzy Logic.* New York: Simon & Schuster, 1993.

Murphy, Nancey and George F.R. Ellis. *On the Moral Nature of the Universe: Theology, Cosmology, and Ethic.* Minneapolis: Fortress Press, 1996.

Murphy, Nancey, Grant Gillett, and John Puddefoot, "What has Theology to Learn from Scientific Methodology." In *Science and Theology: Questions at the Interface,* ed. Murray Rae, Hilary Regan, and John Stenhouse: 101-126. Grand Rapids MI: William B. Eerdmans Publishing Co., 1994.

Murphy, Nancey. "Bridging Theology and Science in a Postmodern Age." In *Bridging Science and Religion,* ed. Ted Peters and Gayman Bennett: 35-46. Minniapolis: Fortress Press, 2003.

________. "The Limits of Pragmatism and the Limits of Realism." *Zygon.* Vol. 28 (1993): 351-359.

________. *Anglo-American Postmodernity: Philosophical Perspectives on Science, Religion, and Ethics.* Colorado: Westview Press, 1997.

________. *Beyond Liberalism and Fundamentalism.* Pennsylvania: Trinity Press International, 1996.

________. *Reconciling Theology and Science: A Radical Reformation Perspective.* Kitchener, Ontario: Pandora Press, 1997.

________. *Theology in the Age of Scientific Reasoning.* Ithaca, NY: Cornell University Press, 1990.

Nathan, T. Pathi. "In Search of Truth through Uncertainty Paradigm." *Convergence.* Vol. 11 (2004): 4-20.

Niekerk, Kees van Kooten. "A Critical Realist Perspective on the Dialogue between Theology and Science." In *Rethinking Theology and Science: Six Models for the Current Dialogue,* ed. Niels Henrik Gregersen and J. Wentzel van Huyssteen: 51-86. Grand Rapids, MI: William B. Eerdmans Publishing Co., 1998.

________. "Critical Realism."In *Encyclopedia of Science and Religion.* 4 Volumes, ed. J. Wentzel Vrede van Huyssteen: 1:190-193. New York: Macmillan/Thomson Gale, 2003.

O'Carrol, Michael. *Trinitas: A Theological Encyclopedia of the Holy Trinity.* Collegeville, Minnesota: The Liturgical Press, 1987.

O'Collins, Gerald. *The Tripersonal God: Understanding and Interpreting the Trinity.* New York: Paulist Press, 1999.

Painadath, S. *We are Co-Pilgrims*, Delhi, ISPCK, 2006.

Panikkar, Raimon. *The Cosmotheandric Experience.* Maryknoll, NY: Orbis Books, 1993.

Pannenberg, Wolfhart. "The Doctrine of Creation and Modern Science." *Zygon: Journal of Religion and Science.* Vol. 23, no. 1 (March 1998): 3-21.

________. "The Doctrine of Creation and Modern Science." In *Cosmos as Creation: Theology and Science in Consonance*, ed. Ted Peters: 152-76, 288. Nashville: Abingdon Press, 1989.

Paul II, John. *Letter to the Reverend George V. Coyne, S.J., Director of Vatican Observatory*, June 1, 1988. In *Physics, Philosophy and Theology: A Common Quest for Understanding*, ed. Robert John Russell, William R. Stoeger and George V. Coyne, S.J.: M 1-M13.Vatican City: Vatican Observatory Publications, 1988.

Peacocke, Arthur. *Intimations of Reality: Critical Realism in Science and Religion.* Notre Dame, IN: University of Notre Dame Press, 1984.

________. *Theology for a Scientific Age: Being and Becoming-Natural, Divine and Human.* Minneapolis: Fortress Press, 1993.

Pedrycz, Witold. *Granular Computing: An Emerging Paradigm.* Heidelberg, Germany: Physica-Verlag, 2001.

Peters, Ted and Carl Peterson. "The Higgs Boson: An Adventure in Critical Realism." *Theology and Science.* Vol. 11, no. 3 (2013): 185-207.

________. "On Creating the Cosmos." In *Physics, Philosophy and Theology: A Common Quest for Understanding*, ed. Robert John Russell, William R. Stoeger, S.J. and George V. Coyne, S.J.: 273-296. Vatican: Vatican Observatory Publications, 1988.

________. *Anticipating Omega: Science, Faith and Our Ultimate Future.* Gottingen: Vandenhoeck & Ruprecht, 2006.

________. *God the World's Future: Systematic Theology for New Era.* 2nd edition. Minneapolis: Fortress Press, 2000.

Piroozfar, Reza. "Search of a Justified Decision-Making Process in Urban Planning." Ph.D. Dissertation. Berlin University of Technology, 2012.

Polkinghorne, John. "Eschatology: Some Questions and Some Insights from Science." In *The End of the World and the Ends of God*, ed. John Polkinghorne and Michael Welker: 29-41. Harrisburg: Trinity Press International, 2000.

________. *Belief in God in an Age of Science*. New Haven, CT: Yale University Press, 1998.

________. *Faith, Science, and Understanding*. New Haven, CT: Yale University Press, 2000.

________. *Scientists as Theologians*. London: Society for Promoting Christian Knowledge, 1996.

________. *Scientists as Theologians: A Comparison of the Writings of Ian G. Barbour, Arthur Peacocke and John Polkinghorne*. London: Society for Promoting Christian Knowledge, 1996.

Popper, Karl. *The Logic of Scientific Discovery*. New York: Routledge, 1977.

Priest, Graham. *An Introduction to Non-Classical Logic: From If to Is*. 2nd edition. Cambridge: Cambridge University Press, 2000.

Quine, Willard V.O. "Two Dogmas of Empiricism." *Philosophical Review*. Vol. 40 (1951): 20-43.

Reddy, P. Venkata Subba. "Fuzzy Modelling and Natural Language Processing for Panini's Sanskrit Grammar." *Journal of Computer Science and Engineering*. Vol. 1, no. 1 (2010): 99-101.

Reese, W. L. "Structuralism." In *Dictionary of Philosophy and Religion*, ed. W. L. Reese: 553. Atlantic Highlands, N.J: Humanities, 1980.

Ross, Timothy J. and W. Jerry Parkinson. "Fuzzy Set Theory, Fuzzy Logic and Fuzzy Systems." In *Fuzzy Logic and Probability Applications: Bridging the Gap*, ed. Timothy J. Ross, Jane M. Booker, W. Jerry Parkinson: 29-54. Philadelphia: Society for Industrial and Applied Mathematics, 2002.

Russell, Robert John. "Contingency in Physics and Cosmology: A Critique of the Theology of Wolfhart Pannenberg." *Zygon.* Vol. 23, no. 1 (1998): 23-43.

________. *Cosmology: From Alpha to Omega.* Minneapolis: Fortress Press, 2008.

________. *Time in Eternity: Pannenberg, Physics and Eschatology in Creative Mutual Interaction.* Notre Dame, Indiana: University of Notre Dame Press, 2012.

Saether, Knut-Willy. *Traces of God: Exploring John Polkinghorne on Theology and Science.* Trondheim, Norway: Tapir Academic Press, 2011.

Singpurwalla, Nozer D. and Jane M. Booker. "Membership Functions and Probability Measures of Fuzzy Sets."*Journal of the American Statistical Association.* Vol. 99, no. 467 (2004): 867-877.

Society of Jesus. "The Intellectual Dimension of Jesuit Ministries." *General Congregation* 34, no. 401. Anand, Gujrat: Gujarat Sahitya Prakash, 1995.

Torrance, Thomas F. *Belief in Science and in Christian Life: The Relevance of Michel Polanyi's Thought for Christian Faith and Life.* Edinburgh: Handsel Press, 1980.

Turksen, Burhan. *An Ontological and Epistemological Perspective of Fuzzy Set Theory.* Amsterdam: Elsevier Science, 2006.

Turunen, Esko. *Mathematics Behind Fuzzy Logic.* Heidelberg: Physica-verlag, 1999.

van Huyssteen, J. Wentzel. *Essays in Postfoundationalist Theology.* Grand Rapids MI: William B. Eerdmans Publishing Co., 1997.

________. *Theology and the Justification of Faith: Constructing Theories in Systematic Theology.* Grand Rapids MI: William B. Eerdmans Publishing Co., 1989.

Vatican II, *Gaudium et Spes,* no. 36.

Walicki, Michat. *Introduction to Mathematical Logic.* Singapore: World Scientific, 2012.

Wilkinson, David. *Christian Eschatology and the Physical Universe.* London: T & T Clark International, 2010.

Wittgenstein, Ludwig. *Philosophical Investigations.* Trans. G.E.M. Anscombe. New York: The MacMillan Company, 1953.

Wright, Nicholas T. *The New Testament and the People of God.* Minneapolis: Fortress Press, 1992.

Zadeh, L.A. 'Fuzzy Sets." *Information and Control.* Vol. 8 (1965): 338-363.

Zimmermann, H. J. *Fuzzy Set Theory and its Applications.* Dordrecht, Netherlands: Kluwer Academic, 2001.